Please return this book to:
BCLA-McCormack School Library
655 Metropolitan Ave
Hyde Park, MA 02136

A VISUAL HISTORY OF
HOUSES AND
CITIES AROUND
THE WORLD

ROSEN

Nuria Cicero

This edition published in 2017 by
The Rosen Publishing Group, Inc.
29 East 21st Street
New York, NY 10010

Library of Congress Cataloging-in-Publication Data

Names: Cicero, Nuria, author.
Title: A visual history of houses and cities around the world / Nuria Cicero.
Description: New York : Rosen Publishing, 2017. | Series: A visual history of the world | Includes bibliographical references
  and index..
Identifiers: LCCN 2016035112 | ISBN 9781499465723 (library bound)
Subjects: LCSH: Cities and towns—History—Juvenile literature.
Classification: LCC HT111 .F38 2017 | DDC 307.7609—dc23
LC record available at https://lccn.loc.gov/2016035112

Manufactured in Malaysia

Metric Conversion Chart

1 inch = 2.54 centimeters; 25.4 millimeters	1 cup = 250 milliliters
1 foot = 30.48 centimeters	1 ounce = 28 grams
1 yard = .914 meters	1 fluid ounce = 30 milliliters
1 square foot = .093 square meters	1 teaspoon = 5 milliliters
1 square mile = 2.59 square kilometers	1 tablespoon = 15 milliliters
1 ton = .907 metric tons	1 quart = .946 liters
1 pound = 454 grams	355 degrees F = 180 degrees Celsius
1 mile = 1.609 kilometers	

©2016 Editorial Sol90
Barcelona – Buenos Aires
All Rights Reserved
Editorial Sol90, S.L

Original Idea Nuria Cicero
Editorial Coordination Alberto Hernández
Editorial Team Alberto Moreno de la Fuente, Luciana Rosende, Virginia Iris Fernández, Pablo Pineau, Matías Loewy, Joan Soriano, Mar Valls, Leandro Jema
Proofreaders Marta Kordon, Edgardo D'Elio
Design María Eugenia Hiriart
Layout Laura Ocampo, Clara Miralles, Paola Fornasaro

Photography Age Fotostock, Getty Images, Science Photo Library, National Geographic, Latinstock, Album, ACI, Cordon Press
Illustrations and Infographics Trexel Animation, Trebol Animation,
WOW Studio, Sebastián Giacobino, Néstor Taylor, Nuts Studio, Steady in Lab, 3DN, Federico Combi, Pablo Aschei, Leonardo César, 4D News, Rise Studio, Ariel Roldán, Dorian Vandegrift, Zoom Desarrollo Digitales, Marcelo Regalado.

Contents

Introduction

For thousands of years, humans have built shelters to find protection from the weather and external dangers. Over time, these shelters became family homes, which were grouped together to form villages and then **cities**. These are one of the most significant elements of civilization: social structure is reflected on its urban layout, the power of great empires, on their palaces; the strength of belief, on its temples... on its stones, there is the footprint that different cultures have left on their way through history.

The great civilizations of **Antiquity** shaped these cities and endowed them with palaces, temples, markets, public squares and administrative buildings. **Urbanism** -planning of urban structure- and architecture changed at the pace of new times. In the European medieval era, cities were characterized by their defensive feature, while in the **East**, they showed all the splendor of their emperors. With Renaissance, they became more humanistic and, during the Baroque period, more monumental. The **Industrial Revolution** of the nineteenth century completely changed the urban landscape. The cities were filled with factories and grew at a rapid pace, while the rail closed the distances between them. A new social class, the proletariat, gathered in neighborhoods in poor condition, while the growing bourgeoisie stayed in private mansions.

Urban growth has not stopped since. In the twentieth century, the **metropolis** and megacities, urban agglomerations of several million people, were formed. New materials and technologies allowed cities to grow upwards and be filled with **skyscrapers**, and downwards, punching the ground to build transport routes, galleries and parking lots. Today, there are over 7,000 million people on the planet and more than half live in cities. Given these data, the challenges of the XXI century will be to make cities more efficient in terms of energy consumption, more environmentally friendly and more liveable.

Chronology

9000 BC

▶ FIRST CITIES

The earliest agricultural villages were first built in the Fertile Crescent. Houses were erected using novel adobe bricks.

3000 BC

▶ EGYPT AND MESOPOTAMIA

The Sumerian and Egyptian cities had temples, palaces and tombs. The dwellings became more complex, with floors and different areas.

6th to 13th century

▶ MIDDLE AGES

In Europe, cities were small and sparsely populated. In contrast, cities in the Islamic world had large palaces and mosques, neighborhoods grouped by professions and active bazaars.

1,500,000 years ago

▶ SHELTERS AND TREES

The earliest hominids took refuge in trees or caves. In the Palaeolithic, caves were used for long periods.

6th to 4th century BC

▶ CLASSICAL GREECE

Religious buildings clustered in the Acropolis, and public spaces in the agora. The houses were simple and had a central courtyard.

1st century BC to 5th century AD

▶ ANCIENT ROME

The Romans built cities with sewers, fountains, aqueducts and bridges. They had two types of housing: the domus and insulae.

14th to 16th century

▶ **RENAISSANCE**
In Europe, the city emerges and becomes a symbol of the growing power of the bourgeoisie. The houses of the artisans are transformed into shops and workshops.

17th to 18th century

▶ **BAROQUE**
The public and administrative buildings loom large and become the benchmark of citizenship.

Twentieth century

▶ **METROPOLISES AND MEGACITIES**
Population growth and technological developments give birth to metropolises and megacities.

▶ **BUILDINGS AND SKYSCRAPERS**
In opposition to the suburbs, houses in height or skyscrapers appeared. New materials: concrete, steel and glass.

9th century BC to 15th century

▶ **PRE-COLUMBIAN AMERICA**
Different civilizations achieve a high level of urbanization, as the Mayans and Aztecs in Mesoamerica, and Tiwanaku, Nazca and Inca people in the south.

15th century

▶ **CHINESE EMPIRE**
The Ming Dynasty built the Forbidden City. In Beijing, the hutong and siheyuan (spacious homes with a central courtyard) multiply.

18th to 19th century

▶ **NEOCLASSICISM**
The architecture is monumental, the main streets are widened and trees, walks, and large squares appear.

19th century

▶ **INDUSTRIAL CITY**
It is divided into very distinct neighborhoods: the proletariat lives in overcrowded and poor conditions near factories; the bourgeoisie enjoys an orderly city with comfortable houses.

21st century

▶ **FUTURISTIC CITY**
The futuristic urbanism aims at anticipating solutions to the negative effects of population growth, environmental degradation and energy crises.

Ancient Times

Chapter 1

More than 50,000 years ago, hominids built shelters from branches and rocks or took advantage of the natural caves for protection against inclement weather. But such provisional shelters were abandoned to continue the search for sustenance. Later, with the so-called Neolithic Revolution, when our ancestors learned to cultivate plants and domesticate animals, the first stable settlements began to appear. These villages made of primitive huts grew until they became small towns with houses made of adobe, different districts and buildings devoted to other tasks, such as storage houses or shrines. From the third millennium BC, Mesopotamian kingdoms and the Egyptian Empire erected imposing cities with temples and palaces, witnesses of their wealth and power. However, it is in classical Greece and then in imperial Rome times when urban planning reaches its highest degree of perfection. Cities are planned according to the needs of public life and its inhabitants; sewers, aqueducts, baths and even housing blocks are constructed to accommodate a growing urban population.

The cave

The use of caves as shelter was characteristic of Western Europe, especially in the areas that are currently Spain and France. Neanderthals and Cro-Magnon were their usual inhabitants in the late Palaeolithic, about 50,000 years ago.

Different spaces

Inside the cave, spaces were separated according to the different activities: areas for working with meat and removing skin, drying areas, quartering areas and spaces for food preservation. The widest area was reserved as a resting place. In the Upper Palaeolithic, small individual cottages were built inside caves.

FIRE
Inside them, a fire was lit which gave warmth and was useful to cook food. At night, this fire kept animals away from the cave.

COMMUNITY LIFE
Family ties were strong. Young kids watched their elders to acquire basic working techniques.

DISTRIBUTION OF TASKS
The activities were distributed among group members: some would hunt, some made tools and the others lit fires.

SOIL
In the Late Palaeolithic, the inside of the cave was perfected. To isolate soil moisture, this was covered with flat stones and leaves.

MAMMOTH BONES CABINS
In Mezhyrich, Ukraine, huts made of mammoth bones were discovered; a finding dating from 15,000 years ago.

Outdoor shelters

With the end of glaciations and the arrival of a mild weather, forests and grasslands proliferated. In these circumstances, the tent or semi-permanent housing appeared, built with mammoth bones, skins and branches. The camps could have several of these larger structures and host to numerous members of one or more families.

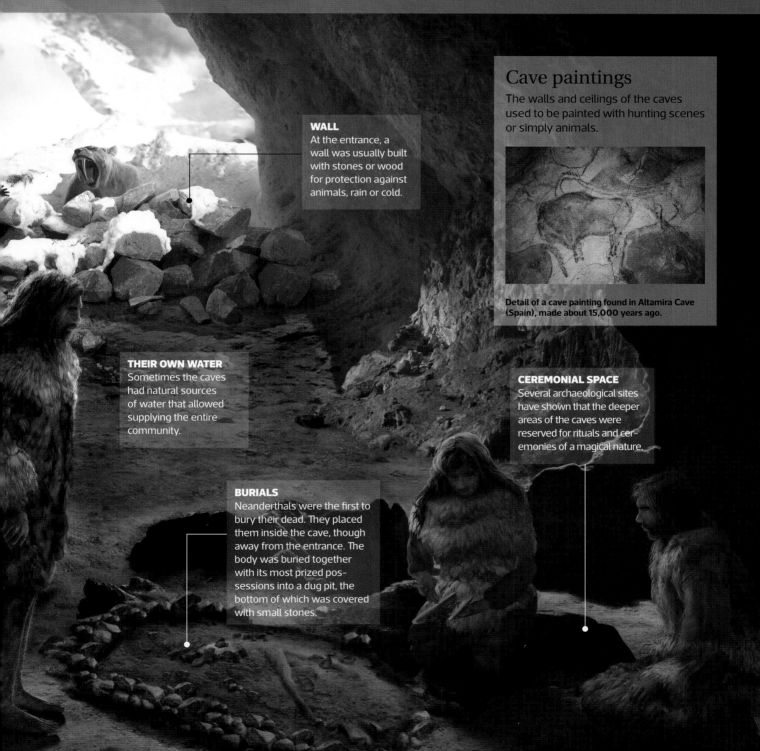

WALL
At the entrance, a wall was usually built with stones or wood for protection against animals, rain or cold.

Cave paintings

The walls and ceilings of the caves used to be painted with hunting scenes or simply animals.

Detail of a cave painting found in Altamira Cave (Spain), made about 15,000 years ago.

THEIR OWN WATER
Sometimes the caves had natural sources of water that allowed supplying the entire community.

CEREMONIAL SPACE
Several archaeological sites have shown that the deeper areas of the caves were reserved for rituals and ceremonies of a magical nature.

BURIALS
Neanderthals were the first to bury their dead. They placed them inside the cave, though away from the entrance. The body was buried together with its most prized possessions into a dug pit, the bottom of which was covered with small stones.

The first settlements

In the Neolithic, with the gradual replacement of hunting and gathering by agriculture and livestock, human groups began to settle in small villages. Many are then transformed into major cities.

From village to large settlement

The first human settlements began around 12,000 years ago as simple groups of about twenty huts, usually of a circular shape, that did not exceed the hundred people. As plants and animals were domesticated, villages grew resulting in large settlements with several thousand inhabitants and in the first cities.

The Fertile Crescent

This name is given to the geographical area stretching from the Nile Valley to Mesopotamia, where the great changes that led to the so-called Neolithic Revolution began. The main archaeological sites of this period are located in this area.

ANATOLIA
Catal Hüyük
● Nevali Çori
● Mureybit
MESOPOTAMIA
Euphrates   Tigris
EGYPT   ARABIA
Nile

3 **Catal Hüyük**
Located in Anatolia and founded around 7000 B.C. Catal Hüyük covered an area of 13 hectares and it had shrines and a complex residential planning.

2 **Nevali Çori**
The village was located surrounding the Euphrates River. Its inhabitants were still hunters, but had begun to grow grains and build food deposits.

1 **Mureybet**
This hunter-gatherer village was located in present-day Syria. It was small and consisted of clusters of houses made of sticks and stones, probably coated with skins for a roof.

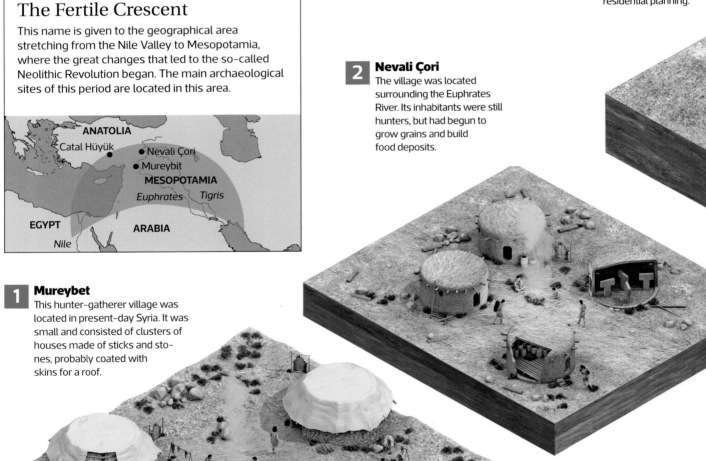

The Neolithic Revolution

The advent of agriculture was a long process that began thousands of years ago towards 9000 BC in the so-called Fertile Crescent. Crops and livestock, along with a sedentary life, provoked major changes in the organization of communities, grouped in growing villages with a division of tasks and labor specialization.

LITHIC CULTURE
During the Neolithic, polished stone tools began being developed, such as axes and arrowheads.

OCCUPATIONS
There were neighborhoods dedicated to specific manufacturing and the production of textiles, and objects of copper, obsidian and bone.

INSIDE
The houses had several rooms. The largest ones had platforms to sit and sleep.

HOUSING
They had rectangular foundation and they were connected together through the roofs. There were no roads.

Chronology

During the Epipaleolithic, with the end of the last glacial period, and the Neolithic progressive human settlements started in the Fertile Crescent region with the emergence of new cultural forms.

1 Natufian and Zarzian Culture
13000-10000 BC
Small villages with huts of rounded shape, and microlithic culture. Harvest of wild cereals.

2 Preceramic Neolithic A
10000-8500 BC
More elaborate housing with adobe walls and compartments. First wall in Jericho.

3 Preceramic Neolithic B
8500-6250 BC
Rectangular housing, development of lithic technology and complex funeral rites.

The Sumerian house

The Sumerians lived in Mesopotamia, present-day Iraq. For its great urban development, they are deemed the first great civilization in history. Taking advantage of the natural resources, they built their home cities with mud bricks dried in the sun.

Major cities

The most striking innovation of the Sumerian civilization was urban planning. In late 3000 BC, 90% of the population of southern Mesopotamia lived in cities. This aroused the admiration and cupidity of the invaders. While the houses were spacious (around 90 m²), they were built close together, one next to the other.

TERRACE
It was common for houses to have walkable ceilings to seize daylight to the most.

WALLS
Walls were smooth and of a whitish color. There were no windows and the rooms had little natural light.

RECEPTION
Next to the front door, a small antechamber pre-served the inside of the house.

Ingenious construction

The first Sumerian houses were cylindrical and built with bundles of dried reeds and rushes. It is believed that they could have been occupied by several families at the same time. At present, this kind of construction remains and it is called *mudhif*.

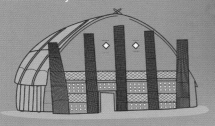

FURNITURE
It was simple, mostly made from wicker. The tables used to be low because they used to sit on the floor. To rest, they would lie on the ground or on simple mats.

CORRIDORS
The two-story homes communicated the higher rooms through a balcony, usually built with firm mats or rushes.

ZIGGURATS
These pyramidal temples were made of several overlapping terraces and a ceremonial enclosure at the top. They could be up to 15 meters high.

THE VALUE OF ADOBE
As stone was scarce in the region and the wood was not very good, the Sumerians used bricks of adobe (a lump of clay). The problem was that the wind and rain would wear them soon.

INSULATION
Adobe bricks kept the heat at night, and also kept the house cool during the hottest days.

CENTRAL SPACE
The houses could be circular or rectangular, but they all had a central open space that allowed for the lighting and ventilation of all the rooms.

DURATION
Foundations were not necessary given the clayey soil. When a building was no longer safe, they would knock it down and build another one on the same site.

KITCHEN
Each house had an area for food preparation. A clay oven was located there to make bread, the basis of their diet. Overall, the meat they consumed was poultry.

Cities of Ancient Egypt

The Egyptian civilization flourished for over 3,000 years around the Nile River. Great cities were erected along its margins, like Memphis and Thebes (modern Luxor), testaments to the power of the Pharaoh and of the devotion to the gods.

Thebes, sacred city

The Greek poet Homer called it "the city of a hundred gates." It was the capital of the Empire and the spiritual and political center between 2055 BC and 1070 BC. When it ceased to be the capital, it kept its feature of the most important holy city of Egypt. It was a busy city with a neighborhood of artisans, a port, to which products and novelties arrived, and a market that supplied the population daily.

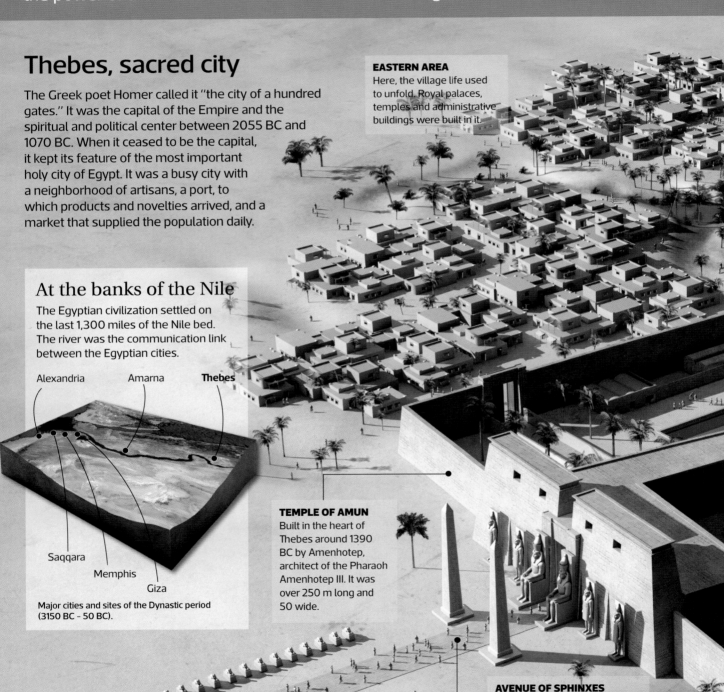

At the banks of the Nile

The Egyptian civilization settled on the last 1,300 miles of the Nile bed. The river was the communication link between the Egyptian cities.

Alexandria   Amarna   **Thebes**

Saqqara

Memphis

Giza

Major cities and sites of the Dynastic period (3150 BC – 50 BC).

EASTERN AREA
Here, the village life used to unfold. Royal palaces, temples and administrative buildings were built in it.

TEMPLE OF AMUN
Built in the heart of Thebes around 1390 BC by Amenhotep, architect of the Pharaoh Amenhotep III. It was over 250 m long and 50 wide.

AVENUE OF SPHINXES
It linked the temple of Thebes with that of Karnak, nearly 3 km away. It is believed that it displayed around 1,350 sphinxes.

THE NILE
Backbone of the Empire. With its floods and waters it fertilized the soil, promoting the flourishing of Egyptian cities.

Structure of cities

Egyptian cities had an elongated shape, following the course of the river. Almost all of them had a main road, which ran parallel to the river bed, and a central square, from which the other streets derived and around which the life of the common people developed, in contrast to that of the nobility and clergy related to palaces and temples.

CARAVANS
The Koptos path was followed to reach Thebes with goods and slaves coming from the Persian Gulf and the Red Sea.

AFRICAN WEALTH
Caravans arrived at Thebes bordering the Nile from Punt, on the African coast of the Indian Ocean, or through the routes of the Sahara desert.

The Egyptian house

The majority of the people of the Ancient Egypt lived in small villages near crop fields. The houses were built with adobe bricks and were home to families comprised by parents, grandparents, uncles and four or five kinds, as an average.

Family unit

The Egyptians invented the living room, where all the family members shared meals, work and spare time. Within these family units, with decorated walls, original furniture was used and they lived together with their pets. The rooms of the house had different purposes and there were also basements and terraces. The windows were placed high on the walls to prevent the direct entry of the sunlight, the soil dust and sand, while wall bricks smeared with bitumen proved impervious to rain.

VENTILATION
These houses counted with vents on the roofs and windows on the upper part of the walls. They were small, rectangular openings without glass. They were protected by stone bars or railings.

RECEPTION HALL
The lobby was the first room of the house, where the people outside the family were received. It used to be intensely decorated since it harbored an altar to honor the god Bes, protector of family, children and pregnant women.

WALLS
The walls were solid combinations of bricks piled up on stone foundations.

FIRST ACCESS
The entrance door was much thicker than those inside, and it counted with a system of safety locks. The doors were made of wood.

The houses of the nobility

The closest relatives to the Pharaoh or the wealthiest Egyptians built houses with large gardens and yards where they grew plants, palm trees and flowers. They even used to create ponds to cool off. Some families chose to have an interior yard in the center of the house to provide luminosity and moderate the heat.

GARDENS
The houses of nobility used to have large gardens and patios with plants and even ponds to cool off.

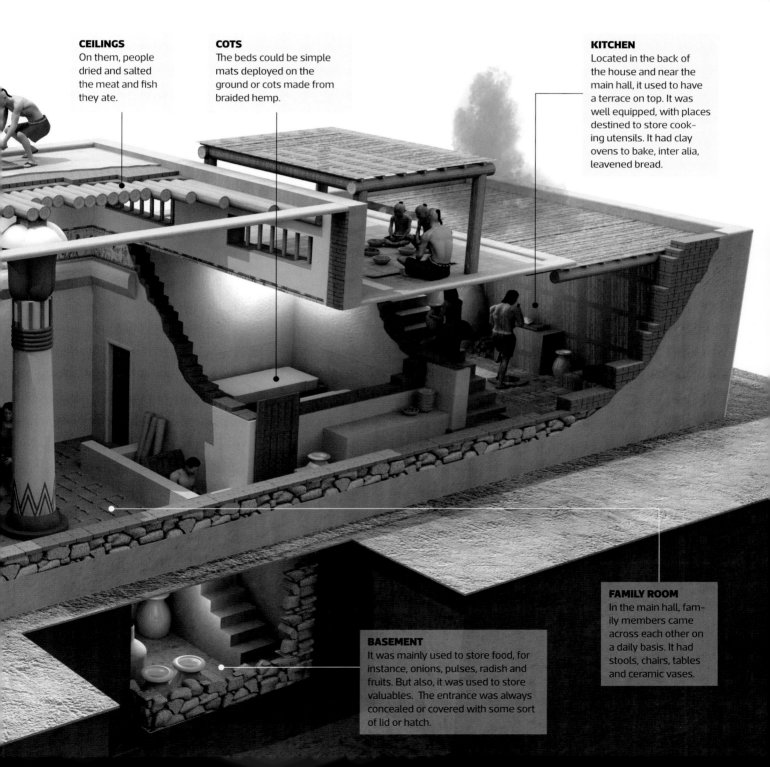

CEILINGS
On them, people dried and salted the meat and fish they ate.

COTS
The beds could be simple mats deployed on the ground or cots made from braided hemp.

KITCHEN
Located in the back of the house and near the main hall, it used to have a terrace on top. It was well equipped, with places destined to store cooking utensils. It had clay ovens to bake, inter alia, leavened bread.

FAMILY ROOM
In the main hall, family members came across each other on a daily basis. It had stools, chairs, tables and ceramic vases.

BASEMENT
It was mainly used to store food, for instance, onions, pulses, radish and fruits. But also, it was used to store valuables. The entrance was always concealed or covered with some sort of lid or hatch.

The splendor of Babylon

Babylon was erected on the banks of the Euphrates River in Mesopotamia more than 4,000 years ago, but reached its maximum splendor in the seventh century BC under the reign of Nebuchadnezzar II. Imperial capital and holy city, its name means "Gate of God."

The New Babylon

For millennia, Babylon was a center of pilgrimage until its complete destruction by the Assyrians circa 689 BC. Reborn under the Neo-Babylonian Empire, it became the greatest city of the Asian Mesopotamia. In the seventh century BC, it was home to approximately 500,000 inhabitants, an extraordinary number of people at the time.

EUPHRATES RIVER
It ran through the city dividing it into two areas. The inside counter-walls ran along both banks.

PARALLEL STREETS
Its layout was of straight streets, either parallel or perpendicular to the river. At the end of each street there was a bronze postern.

PROCESSION AVENUE
Main road of Babylon. It extended from the Ishtar Gate to Esagila, the temple complex surrounding the Etemenanki.

ISHTAR GATE
Decorated with glazed bricks and images of lions and griffins, it was the most beautiful gate of Babylon.

Urban design

In times of Nebuchadnezzar II, the city had a rectangular shape; it was strongly walled and divided in two by the Euphrates River.

Ishtar Gate

Etemenanki

Euphrates River

Legendary city

Babylon was located in a large plain, forming a square with a perimeter of about 17 km. It was encircled by a deep and broad pit, full of water, and a double wall that was 25 m wide and 12 m high. Said pit was defended by casemates and, according to the Greek historian Herodotus, it had a hundred gates, all made of bronze.

TEMPLES AND GARDENS
With its 53 temples, 955 small shrines and 384 street altars, Babylon was an unrivalled religious center. Legend also attributes it the hanging gardens, one of the Seven Wonders of the Ancient World for the Greeks.

THE ETEMENANKI
This ziggurat, having a foundation of 90 m of width and more than 90 m of height, counted with seven levels.

HANGING GARDENS
According to legend, Nebuchadnezzar II ordered their construction in 600 BC and they were destroyed by earthquakes in the second century BC.

ROYAL PALACE
It was a palace complex or inner city that housed temples, palaces and houses.

BRICKS
Those for walls were yellow; those for gates, light blue; for palaces, pink; and for temples, white.

The grid plan

The layout of orthogonal type that organizes the urban plan with straight streets intersecting at right angles, creating rectangular blocks, has its origins in Ancient Times. In Classical Greece, it became a paradigm that was eventually applied in the world.

From Miletus

The idea of orthogonal planning was wielded by Hippodamus (498–408 BC), a Greek architect who designed the reconstruction of his home city, Miletus. His urbanization plan, known as "grid plan" would later be a feature of multiple cities. The Romans perfected and implemented it in all their expansions. It was relegated in the Middle Ages, but it regained momentum in the sixteenth century and especially in the seventeenth century, when the Spanish monarchy regulated the design of its American colonies. Over time, the cities incorporated diagonal streets and avenues to their orthogonal design that benefited circulation.

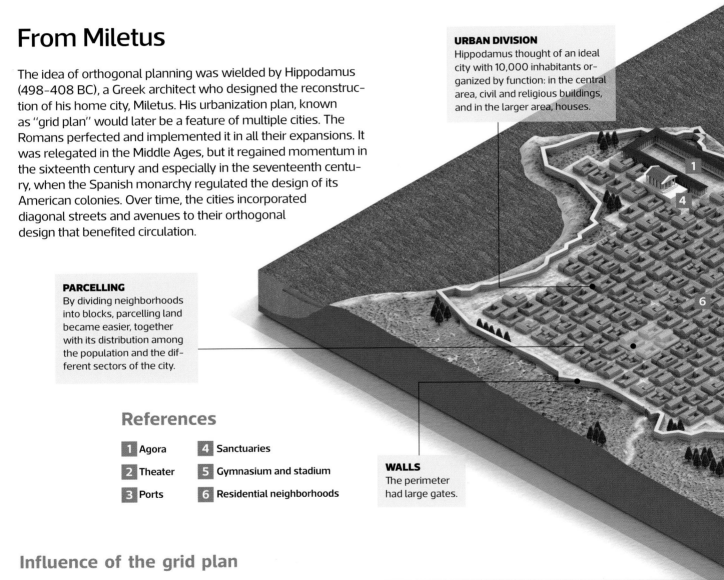

URBAN DIVISION
Hippodamus thought of an ideal city with 10,000 inhabitants organized by function: in the central area, civil and religious buildings, and in the larger area, houses.

PARCELLING
By dividing neighborhoods into blocks, parcelling land became easier, together with its distribution among the population and the different sectors of the city.

WALLS
The perimeter had large gates.

References

1	Agora	**4**	Sanctuaries
2	Theater	**5**	Gymnasium and stadium
3	Ports	**6**	Residential neighborhoods

Influence of the grid plan

I Century BC	XVII Century	1811

Ancient Rome
The Romans took the Greek legacy. They incorporated wider roadways than the rest of the streets, which crossed the city, for better circulation.

Colonial America
The Laws of the Indies contemplated the construction of cities with a grid plan. Lima is one of them. The main buildings were built around the central square.

The cities of Hippodamus

At the time of Pericles, the Greek pioneer of urban development, Hippodamus, applied his idea of orthogonal city planning to Piraeus (map) port of the ancient city of Athens. Also, he was the architect who designed the Greek colony of Thurii, on the Gulf of Taranto, after its founding by the ruins of Sybaris in 444 BC.

PIRAEUS AND MORE
It is believed that Hippodamus also applied his urban planning skills for the organization of the city of Rhodes.

TOPOGRAPHICAL ADAPTATION
Given the existence of two bays, Hippodamus placed public and religious buildings in the center between them, and the residential neighborhoods on both sides.

LONG PATHS
This type of grid plan was orderly, but required to travel longer distances. There were no shortcuts or diagonal streets.

INTERSECTIONS
Blocks with square angles impeded visibility at intersections, which caused accidents.

BOULEUTERION
Where the council of nobles met.

SOUTHERN AGORA
It articulates the two urban traces in which the peninsula is divided.

Other urban plans

CONCENTRIC MODEL
The radial streets converge and communicate other streets among each other. Parcelling is complicated.

IRREGULAR
Without a defined shape, it is often the result of urban sprawl. It was common in medieval Islamic cities.

LINEAR
It was first developed with an elongated shape that later, when extended, gets lost. It arises parallel to a road, river or other transport means.

> **XIX Century**

> **1945–present**

Orthogonal Manhattan
Its urban growth was planned with a perfect grid: 11 avenues range from north to south and the Island and 155 streets cut them at right angles. en ángulos rectos.

Eixample
The expansion of the limits of Barcelona beyond the urban area was made as a grid. Diagonal streets were incorporated and corners were chamfered.

Rebuilding Europe
After World War II, several cities such as Le Havre (France) had to be rebuilt. The orthogonal layout was implemented on them.

Cities of Ancient Greece

The polis or city-states of ancient Greece were its own economic and political entities. They took on a special significance in public life around the acropolis, religious center, and the agora, main focus of the civil, institutional and commercial life.

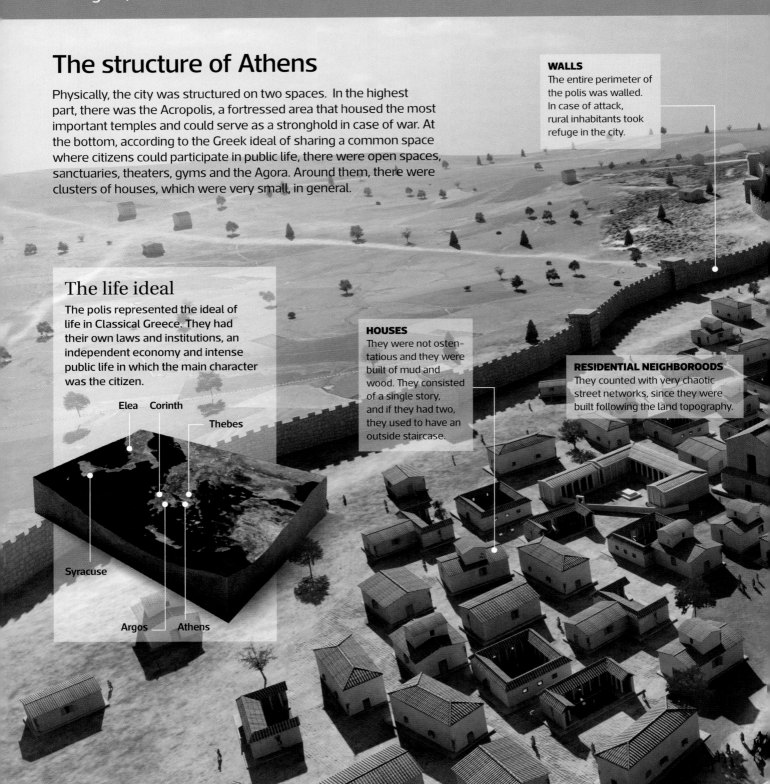

The structure of Athens

Physically, the city was structured on two spaces. In the highest part, there was the Acropolis, a fortressed area that housed the most important temples and could serve as a stronghold in case of war. At the bottom, according to the Greek ideal of sharing a common space where citizens could participate in public life, there were open spaces, sanctuaries, theaters, gyms and the Agora. Around them, there were clusters of houses, which were very small, in general.

The life ideal

The polis represented the ideal of life in Classical Greece. They had their own laws and institutions, an independent economy and intense public life in which the main character was the citizen.

Elea   Corinth

Thebes

Syracuse

Argos   Athens

WALLS
The entire perimeter of the polis was walled. In case of attack, rural inhabitants took refuge in the city.

HOUSES
They were not osten-tatious and they were built of mud and wood. They consisted of a single story, and if they had two, they used to have an outside staircase.

RESIDENTIAL NEIGHBOROODS
They counted with very chaotic street networks, since they were built following the land topography.

CELEBRATIONS

Procession of water-men during the Panathenaic Games, religious festivals dedicated to the goddess Athena. They were carried out every year in the city of Athens.

Pericles (495 BC - 429 BC)

He was the most important statesman for Classical Athens and determinant for the city to reach its maximum splendor, strengthening its political and cultural features.

Athens. It was the epitome of the ideal life of the Greek polis. It had its heyday during the V century BC, when it reached a population of 500,000 inhabitants.

ACROPOLIS

The Acropolis of Athens, located 156 m high on a limestone plateau, was destroyed in 480 BC by the Persians. Pericles ordered the erection of a new Acropolis and called great architects for the task.

STOA

The most significant area of the Agora, where merchants had their stores. Athenians conversed on their porches.

AGORA

It occupied a large area and grouped important temples and commercial and institutional buildings.

The Greek house

Around 300 BC, the most powerful Greek families built comfortable and spacious homes known as *oikos*. They could count with one or two stories and they used to be sober, as they were designed to meet the basic needs of its inhabitants.

Internal layout

The homes of wealthy families responded to a planned distribution, in which each of the rooms was intended for a specific use: there were areas of service, reception, bedrooms, kitchen and rooms for the hygiene. Later, this division of spaces was adopted by the Romans and spread through Europe. The Greek civilization laid the foundations of Western housing up to present day.

OPENINGS
The windows were few and located high to protect the privacy of the family. The openings were simple square or round holes. In days of cold or strong winds, they were covered with wood or fabrics.

Expansions

Originally, the houses of the Greek polis were very basic and counted with one sole multifunctional room. Throughout the centuries, the rooms multiplied themselves and became larger by their mere juxtaposition, and they incorporated a central yard or vegetable garden that provided luminosity and ventilation.

Ruins of a house in the Greek city of Mystras, near Sparta.

GYNOECIUM
Reserved for women and children, placed on the top floor, in a place of difficult access.

MATERIALS
The most prominent materials were adobe and wood, which notably distinguished houses from the huge public buildings made of marble and stone.

Housing for poor families

The Greek cities did not abide by a regulating urban plan. Thus, each owner built his house according to his possibilities. The poor sectors built small houses without any organization since the number and the distribution of the rooms depended on the accidents and the extension of the ground they had available.

WOMEN AREA
In the gynoecium, mothers managed the house and educated their children.

ANDRON
Area reserved for men. Where visits were received and feasts or symposiums were held. Delicacies were placed in front of each guest, who seated on stools.

HYGIENE
The houses had washing rooms with hot stone or brick baths. These were filled with water from the well and emptied manually.

HOME-MADE FOOD
The meals were prepared in an area for cooking and food storage. The poor elaborated the food in a portable brazier and on public sidewalks.

ENTRANCE
The house was entered through a single door, made of wood and bolted with a lock, which faced the open central yard.

INTERNAL YARD
The rooms were distributed around a central yard which provided luminosity and ventilation. This open space, common to the entire family, housed a sacrificial altar for the family gods.

Overlapping cities

An urban center can arise from the growth of a village located in an uninhabited area, or be erected on the ruins of an old city, using its remains or simply building on the same location. Troy is the best example of an overlapping city.

The strata of Troy

In 1870, businessman and archaeologist Heinrich Schliemann began excavating Hisarlik Hill, in modern Turkey. His eagerness to find the legendary city described by Homer in the *Iliad* revealed the history of urban development divided into nine strata: from a poor original nucleus dating from the third century BC, to a majestic Roman-style city of the first century of the Christian era. Throughout the centuries, natural disasters and the historical evolution of the various populations caused the abandonment or destruction of Troy once and again, for it to be later reborn with other features.

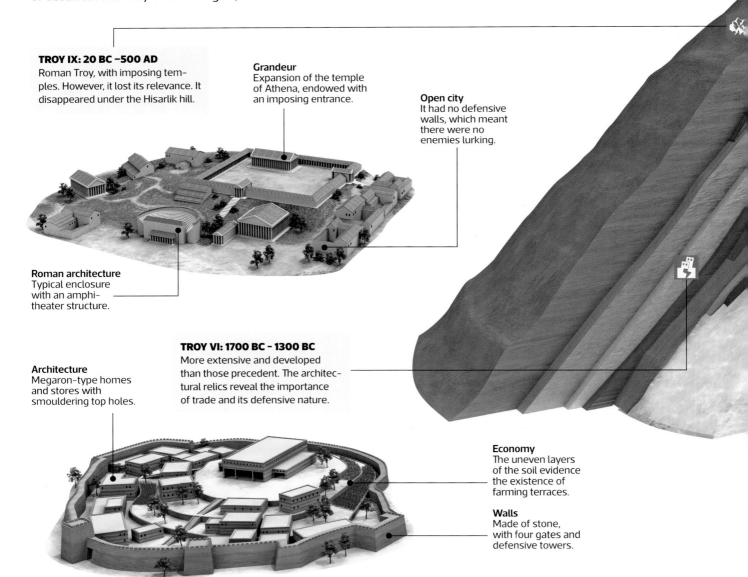

TROY IX: 20 BC –500 AD
Roman Troy, with imposing temples. However, it lost its relevance. It disappeared under the Hisarlik hill.

Grandeur
Expansion of the temple of Athena, endowed with an imposing entrance.

Open city
It had no defensive walls, which meant there were no enemies lurking.

Roman architecture
Typical enclosure with an amphitheater structure.

TROY VI: 1700 BC – 1300 BC
More extensive and developed than those precedent. The architectural relics reveal the importance of trade and its defensive nature.

Architecture
Megaron-type homes and stores with smouldering top holes.

Economy
The uneven layers of the soil evidence the existence of farming terraces.

Walls
Made of stone, with four gates and defensive towers.

Other overlapping cities

In America, there are many examples of cities erected by the Spanish conquistadors on the ruins of pre-Columbian cities such as Tenochtitlan. Christian churches were built on local temples as a form of cultural domination.

NUMANTIA
Excavations revealed the existence of three overlapping cities under this Celtiberian-Roman city located in Cerro de la Muela, in the municipality of Garray within the city of Soria, Spain.

TROY VIII: 700 BC - 85 BC
Hellenic Troy without walls and with great development of religious architecture. A Doric temple of Athena is erected.

TROY VII: 1200 BC - 950 BC
Usually divided into two stages: a brief one, using the ruins of the precedent city, and another stage, inhabited by Indo-European Achaeans.

OLDEST LAYER

BEDROCK

TROY III, IV AND V: 2250-2200 BC; 2200-1900 BC; 1900-1700 BC
Successive settlements. There was no great progress of the architectural features, nor of the walls.

TROY I: 2950 -2350 BC
Small town with precarious buildings. Usage of stone tools.

TROY II: 2350-2250 BC
Overlaid on the first one. It had larger dimensions and Megaron buildings, with a large hall divided into three parts.

References

STRATA

■ Troy IX: 20 BC – 500 AD		■ Troy IV: 2200-1900 BC	
■ Troy VIII: 700-85 BC		■ Troy III: 2250-2200 BC	
■ Troy VII: 1200-950 BC		■ Troy II: 2350-2250 BC	
■ Troy VI: 1700 -1300 BC		■ Troy I: 2950 -2350 BC	
■ Troy V: 1900-1700 BC			

POSSIBLE CAUSES OF DESTRUCTION

 Fire

 Earthquake

 Abandonment

Cities of the Roman Empire

In imperial times (27 BC–476) a vast network of interconnected cities was built. These cities had public buildings with administrative, political, religious and recreational functions, and infrastructure for better quality of life.

Rome, practicality and comfort

At its peak, Rome grew to about one million inhabitants. Like all cities of the empire, besides temples, amphitheaters, public baths, markets or stores, it counted with a sewage system by aqueducts and fountains, paved streets and even fire and police services.

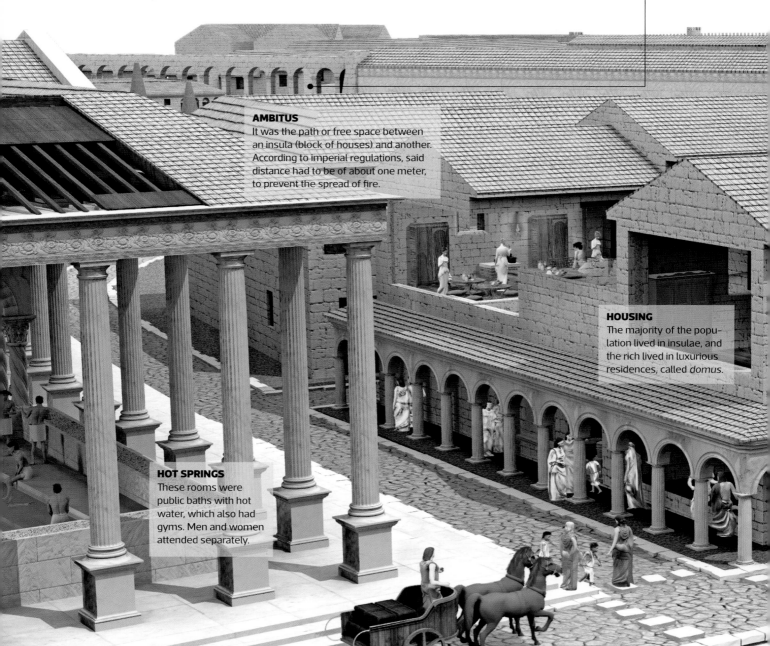

AQUEDUCTS
Major engineering works that allowed carrying a constant flow of water from the mountains to the city.

AMBITUS
It was the path or free space between an insula (block of houses) and another. According to imperial regulations, said distance had to be of about one meter, to prevent the spread of fire.

HOUSING
The majority of the population lived in insulae, and the rich lived in luxurious residences, called *domus*.

HOT SPRINGS
These rooms were public baths with hot water, which also had gyms. Men and women attended separately.

The new urban design

The new provincial cities were designed according to a standard model based on a rectangular layout. They had two main, wide streets that ran across the entire city: the cardo, a north–south-oriented street and the decumanus, which ran east to west. At the intersection of the cardo and decumanus, the forum was located. The remaining lanes were narrower and they formed blocks.

ROMAN FORUM
With gates on three sides and a large temple in the fourth, the Forum was the axis of Rome. There, the Senate met, people voted, justice was imparted and business was done.

TEMPLES
They housed the statues of the gods they worshipped. The Capitol was the religious center of the city.

From village to an imperial capital

Rome grew: it grew from a small village into a mighty imperial capital. In the beginning, it followed the Greek and Etruscan urban parameters, and it grew without much order, adapting to the terrain. During the imperial era, the city grew following a grid plan, that is to say, around major public buildings and monuments of the city center.

Tiber River

Aqueduct

Circus Maximus

Coliseum

STREETS
Paved or covered with slabs. On both sides, there were ditches to prevent flooding.

STORES
There were craft workshops and taverns that opened onto the street, where many products were sold.

SEWERS
The wastewater was led to the sea through a network of underground vaulted galleries.

Roman insula

The need for housing for a growing population from the cities led the Romans to the construction of the first house blocks, the insulae, the precedents of modern buildings.

Humble houses

Each insula occupied a block, usually had five stories and counted with a large number of apartments of different sizes. They were small and uncomfortable spaces inhabited by the poorest sectors of the population. The rooms lacked a set function; therefore, any room could be used to eat or sleep, there were no sanitary facilities and a brazier was used to cook.

WINDOWS AND BALCONIES
The openings, only sources of ventilation and light, were small and protected by wooden shutters. Some apartments counted with very narrow balconies.

Rich houses

The *domus* were luxurious and comfortable residences with several rooms occupied by the wealthiest families. These were organized around an axis, from the vestibule to the peristyle. In the middle, there was the atrium, heart of the house. There were areas reserved for guests and for the exclusive use of the family.

Roman atrium. It was a covered patio that used to have an opening in the center of the roof to collect rainwater.

RENTS
The powerful Romans invested in the construction of insulae and then rented the apartments at a very high price.

MATERIALS
The first insulae were built with wood and adobe, the cheapest materials. However, the frequent collapses and fires led to the application of bricks and concrete.

Living in danger

The insulae were very precarious. The habitual collapses and fires led to the creation of fire-fighter groups and the establishment of safety measures, such as limitations to the number of stories.

STORIES
The stories were communicated by wooden stairs. The apartments on the first floor were bigger and more expensive than those above. In general, they were destined to commercial purposes.

STORES
The commercial shops or taverns were located on the ground floor.

WASTE
Overcrowding and dirt were common. Residues and human waste were accumulated in recipients that were later thrown through the windows.

The Celtic forts

The Celts constituted rural communities spread through large parts of northern Europe between the sixth century BC and the fourth century AD. Their settlements were small walled villages with several buildings, called forts.

Family dwellings

The forts were characterized by their lack of urban organization and by the predominantly cylindrical shapes of all buildings made of wood and stones. They housed several buildings destined to residence and storage. The houses belonged to independent households and they did not share dividing walls, while the deposits could be common spaces.

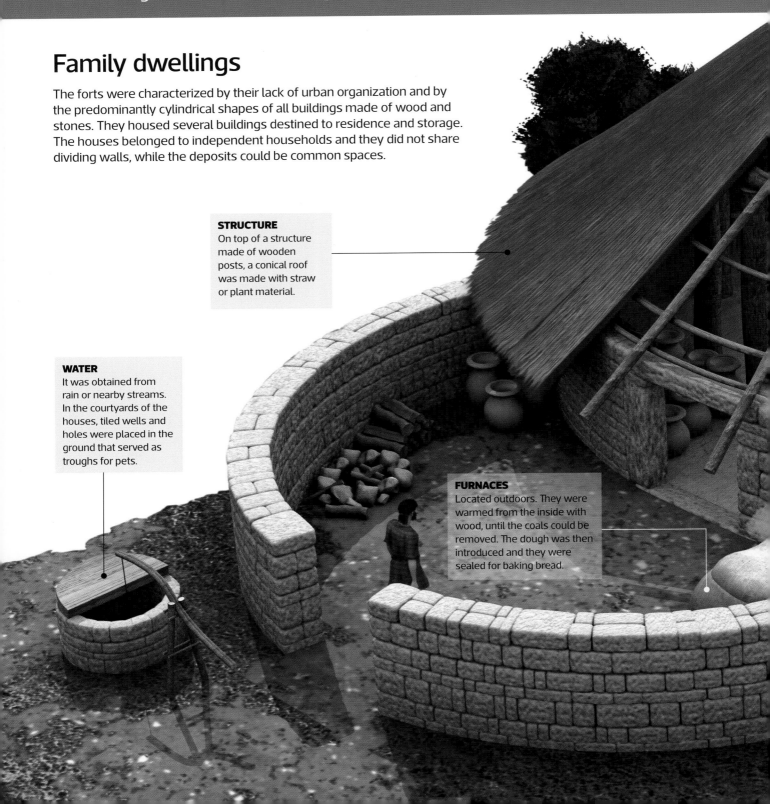

STRUCTURE
On top of a structure made of wooden posts, a conical roof was made with straw or plant material.

WATER
It was obtained from rain or nearby streams. In the courtyards of the houses, tiled wells and holes were placed in the ground that served as troughs for pets.

FURNACES
Located outdoors. They were warmed from the inside with wood, until the coals could be removed. The dough was then introduced and they were sealed for baking bread.

NEIGHBORHOODS
It is the name given to the set of constructions that corresponded to a single family.

FURNITURE
They used very few pieces of furniture to better seize the space. Sometimes, the tables were just earth mounds located next to one of the inner walls of the house.

Interior layout
Although these houses had a single room, they had a specific distribution for the development of the various daily activities.

Personal items
Bedroom
Bedroom
Kitchen
Public area
Work area
Storage area

SOIL
It was prepared with a lower layer of stones and a higher one with rammed clay.

FIREPLACE
Located in the center of the house, it was used for cooking and for heating the room. To cook, the pots were supported with ropes tied to wooden sticks.

Middle and Modern Ages

Chapter 2

The end of the Roman Empire marked the beginning of the Middle Ages in Europe. The feudal system and the division of territory in manors, led to a predominance of rural life and the construction of walled citadels where the priority was defence. Meanwhile, the Islamic empire flourished in the Middle East with cities of narrow streets filled with mosques and bazaars. In Asia, nomadic peoples roamed the steppes with their practical and movable houses from the beginning of the second millennium and the Chinese emperors showed all their power in the Forbidden City, built in the fifteenth century. Around the same time, pre-Columbian American civilizations had large cities with wide roads, pyramids and temples. The Aztec Tenochtitlan (fourteenth century) or the Inca Machu Picchu (fifteenth century) are just a few of its advanced urban development and construction techniques.

In the fifteenth century, the spirit of the Renaissance spread from Italy throughout Europe renewing architecture and urbanism under the paradigm of classical aesthetics and the rule of reason. The streets widened, large squares were opened and the new wealthy sectors (merchants and bankers) built mansions and palaces. Then the absolutist kings of the seventeenth century made their capitals reflect their power, with monumental palaces, gardens and boulevards.

Cities in the Middle Ages

With the fall of the Roman Empire, the cities suffered a process of depopulation, and many disappeared. The population leaving the cities disseminated around rural areas, resulting in agrarian societies over which the feudal regime settled.

Carcassonne, the epitome

The European Middle Ages commenced as a rudimentary rural society upon which the feudal system dominated the social and economic organization. The city was reborn in the eleventh century, driven by a growing bourgeois society, linked to trade and industry. They were small cities, with no more than 20,000 inhabitants, walled and formed by labyrinthine alleys. Carcassonne, in France, is the most representative city. During its 2,500 years of history, it was inhabited by Gaul, Roman, Arab and French people. The citadel was built in 1240 by King Louis IX, and it was a strategic point on the border with the Kingdom of Aragon. In the seventeenth century it lost its military relevance.

WALLS
Defensive Carcassonne is surrounded by a double wall crenellated and defended by 52 towers with conical tops.

In French territory
During the Middle Ages various cities flourished across France. Several of them were in the south, close to Carcassonne.

Bordeaux   Carcassonne

Toulouse   Castelnaudary

PRINCELY CASTLE
Preceded by a large semi-circular barbican, which was the first obstacle for the enemy that had penetrated into the enclosure of the citadel, and a pit. It has an inner courtyard with nine towers.

Circular cities

During the Middle Ages, fights between feudal lords, princes and kingdoms were frequent. For a better defence, cities were built on rocky terrain, meanders, plateaus, etc. Thus, the foundation of medieval cities was circular and had a concentric grid, with the cathedral, the city hall and the market square in the center.

MEDIEVAL ICONS
Other highly representative cities of the Middle Ages are Dubrovnik (image) and the Krak des Chevaliers (current Syria).

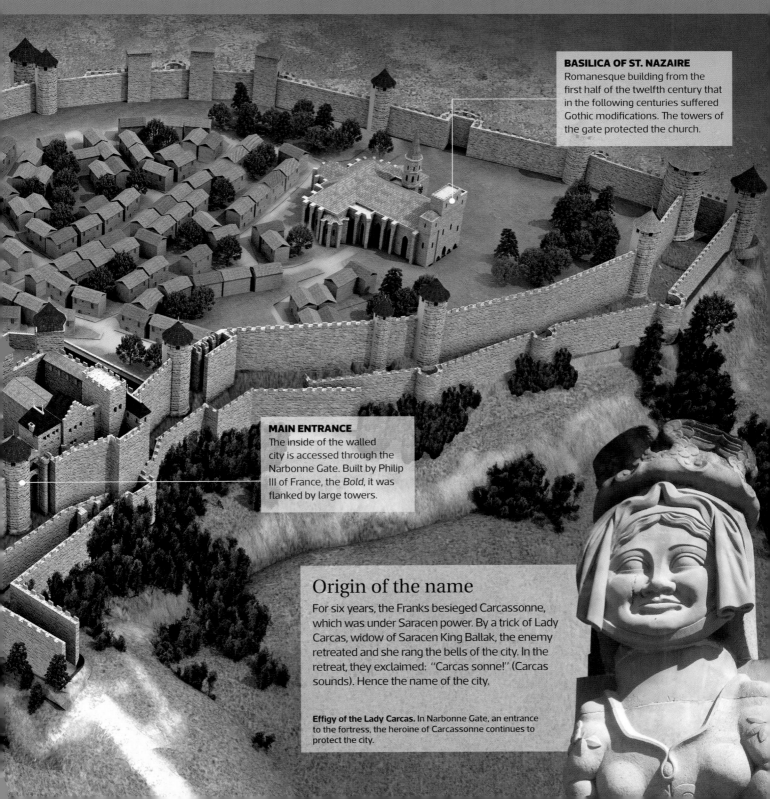

BASILICA OF ST. NAZAIRE
Romanesque building from the first half of the twelfth century that in the following centuries suffered Gothic modifications. The towers of the gate protected the church.

MAIN ENTRANCE
The inside of the walled city is accessed through the Narbonne Gate. Built by Philip III of France, the *Bold*, it was flanked by large towers.

Origin of the name

For six years, the Franks besieged Carcassonne, which was under Saracen power. By a trick of Lady Carcas, widow of Saracen King Ballak, the enemy retreated and she rang the bells of the city. In the retreat, they exclaimed: "Carcas sonne!" (Carcas sounds). Hence the name of the city.

Effigy of the Lady Carcas. In Narbonne Gate, an entrance to the fortress, the heroine of Carcassonne continues to protect the city.

The medieval house

Most medieval houses in Europe were mononuclear, i.e., they consisted of a single room where all daily activities took place. Gradually, the privileged sectors differentiated the domestic spaces.

The barn house

The houses of medieval peasants were simple and small. Built by the family group, they were erected using the materials in the area. They were, at the same time, a sitting area, kitchen, storage room and workshop. The members of one or more families lived together with food, tools and farm animals.

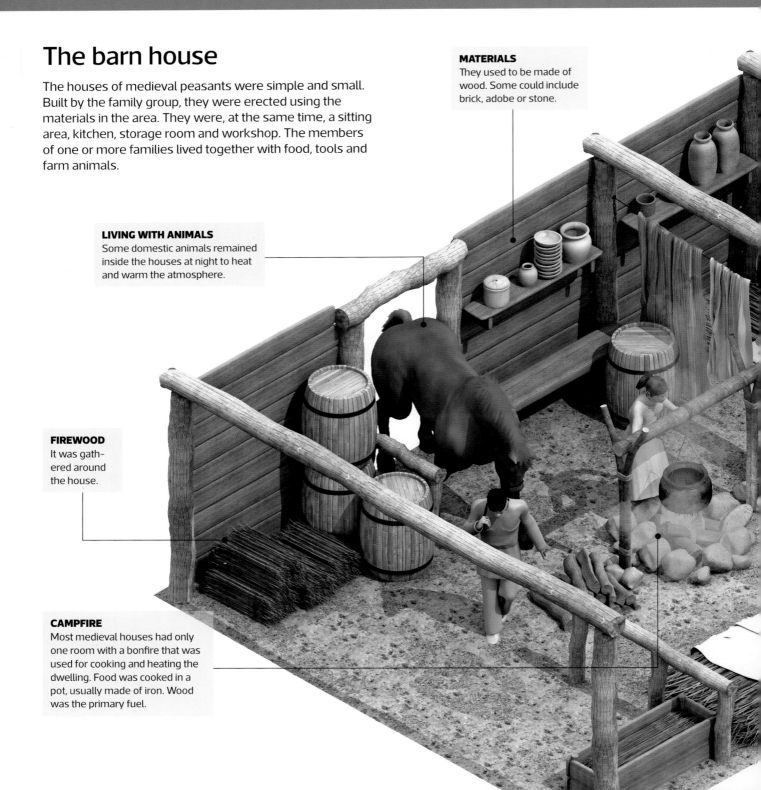

MATERIALS
They used to be made of wood. Some could include brick, adobe or stone.

LIVING WITH ANIMALS
Some domestic animals remained inside the houses at night to heat and warm the atmosphere.

FIREWOOD
It was gathered around the house.

CAMPFIRE
Most medieval houses had only one room with a bonfire that was used for cooking and heating the dwelling. Food was cooked in a pot, usually made of iron. Wood was the primary fuel.

Privacy in the home

The idea of privacy was absent in the construction of houses up to modern and contemporary times. The European Renaissance individualism gradually introduced the concept of intimacy, but it was not until the twentieth century when the custom of separating the bedrooms of spouses from that of children consolidated definitively.

URBAN HOUSING
In cities, the houses used to have two storeys. On the ground floor, the workshop or store and the kitchen were located, and in the second storey, the rooms. They could also have a cellar and a barn.

FURNITURE
The pieces of furniture were sparse. The basic furniture was made up of a bed or cot, table, chairs or benches and chests where clothes, utensils or food were kept.

Large families

Families used to have a large number of members. The married couple, children and a large group of relatives such as widows, orphans, nephews or uncles used to live in the same house.

Preserving the bed

In the late Middle Ages, the use of beds became widespread among powerful sectors, though not always located in rooms exclusively devoted to rest. Also, beds with curtains and the "box-bed," a cot enclosed in a wooden trunk, were common. Slowly, the concept of privacy was imposed.

Beds with curtains. The bed, which could be located or not in an exclusive room, was complemented with the addition of columns, ornaments and curtains at the beginning of the Modern Age.

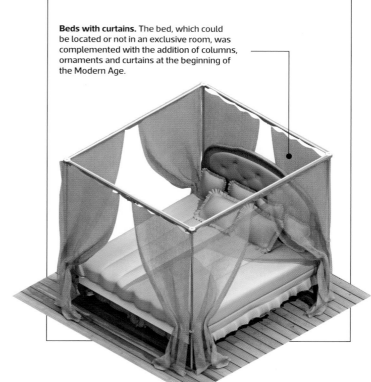

RESTING
They rested together on the floor covered with straw and neared their bodies to keep warm overnight.

Jerusalem, the holy city

Holy city for Christians, Jews and Muslims, Jerusalem would go through a golden age led by the Umayyad caliphs in the seventh and eighth centuries. Palaces, temples and mosques were erected, while the streets were often filled with pilgrims.

The urban layout

In the Islamic world, the private space prevailed over the public: neither the street nor the squares were gathering places. Hence the bare walls and the labyrinths of narrow streets. Public life was concentrated around the mosques, which had their own preponderant space, and markets, which were almost a city within the city. Jerusalem, under Muslim rule, acquired that profile.

HOUSING
The buildings were very simple, with one or two storeys built with stone bricks.

CHRISTIAN AREA
Located around the Church of the Holy Sepulchre and the Via Dolorosa, places revered by Christianity.

Before and after

King Solomon consecrated the First Temple in the tenth century BC. Around this site, the Old City would grow, walled and divided into four quarters.

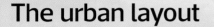

It was of King Solomon

Temple

Royal Palace

Old Town today

Haram Al-Sharif

Ancient city

The footprint of the Umayyad

In 638, the Byzantines surrendered to the armies of Caliph Omar and Jerusalem was on Muslim hands. From 661 until 750, the Umayyad dynasty strengthened Islam and turned it into an actual empire. Under their rule, the capital of Islam moved from Medina to the city of Damascus, and Jerusalem became the third most important holy city.

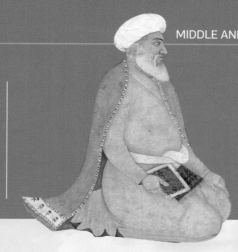

RELIGIOUS RESPECT
When followers of Caliph Omar took the city, they respected the points considered sacred by Jews and Christians.

WALLS AND GATES
The walls were destroyed and rebuilt many times. Its area is about 4.5 km and its height varies between 5 and 15 m, with a thickness of 3 m. Said walls have 43 watch towers and 8 gates.

ISLAMIC AREA
The Muslims gathered around the west and north walls of the sacred esplanade called Haram al Sharif.

Sacred buildings

At the time of Islamic rule, where the Dome of the Rock was imposed on the landscape, other sacred buildings were also erected in Jerusalem.

Church of the Holy Sepulchre

Dome of the Rock

The Citadel El Qal'a

Al-Aqsa Mosque

SACRED PLACE
The Dome of the Rock was the first Islamic building in the city. Built in 691 by the Umayyad caliph Abd al-Malik, where, historically, the Temple of Solomon was placed.

FOUNDATIONS
So strong and resilient that they even protected the Dome of the Rock during the earthquake of 747.

JEWISH AREA
The Caliph Omar allowed the return of the Jews, which led to the rapid development of an important Jewish community, clustered near the Wailing Wall.

Pre-Columbian cities

The Mesoamerican peoples (Olmec, Maya, Teotihuacan, Tarascan, Zapotec, Mixtec and Aztecs) developed a planned urban architecture, in which the religion and the stratification of their societies were expressed in their buildings.

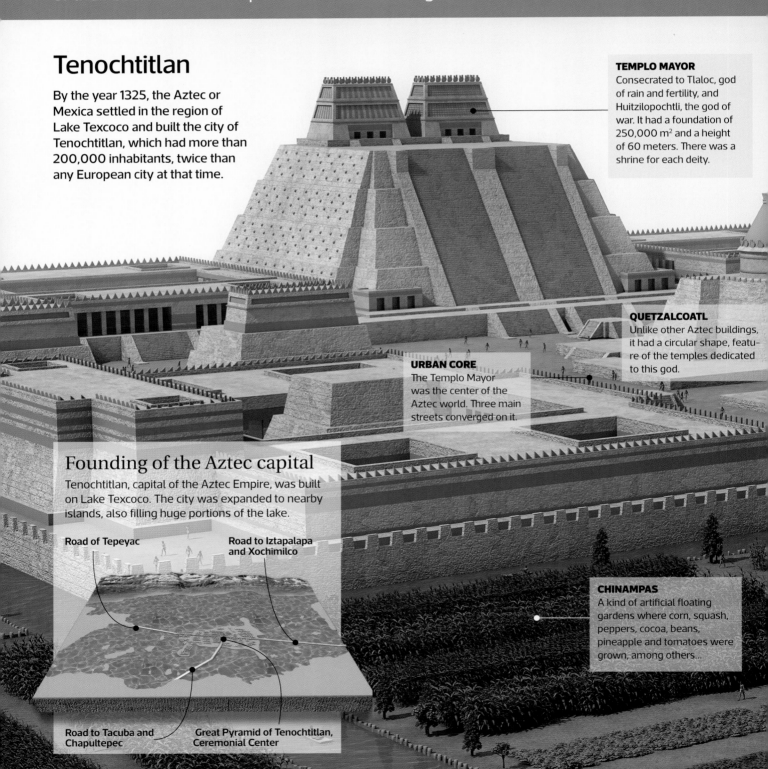

Tenochtitlan

By the year 1325, the Aztec or Mexica settled in the region of Lake Texcoco and built the city of Tenochtitlan, which had more than 200,000 inhabitants, twice than any European city at that time.

TEMPLO MAYOR
Consecrated to Tlaloc, god of rain and fertility, and Huitzilopochtli, the god of war. It had a foundation of 250,000 m² and a height of 60 meters. There was a shrine for each deity.

QUETZALCOATL
Unlike other Aztec buildings, it had a circular shape, feature of the temples dedicated to this god.

URBAN CORE
The Templo Mayor was the center of the Aztec world. Three main streets converged on it.

Founding of the Aztec capital

Tenochtitlan, capital of the Aztec Empire, was built on Lake Texcoco. The city was expanded to nearby islands, also filling huge portions of the lake.

Road of Tepeyac

Road to Iztapalapa and Xochimilco

CHINAMPAS
A kind of artificial floating gardens where corn, squash, peppers, cocoa, beans, pineapple and tomatoes were grown, among others...

Road to Tacuba and Chapultepec

Great Pyramid of Tenochtitlan, Ceremonial Center

Other pre-Columbian cities

Cuzco and Machu Picchu in Peru, Tiwanaku in Bolivia, and Cahokia in the United States, were also big cities. Tikal, in the picture, was one of the most powerful Maya city–states, reaching its peak between 200 and 900 AD.

TEOTIHUACAN
It was located in Mexico and was baptised as "the city of the gods." With their pyramids, it came to have an area of 21 km², and between 100,000 and 200,000 inhabitants.

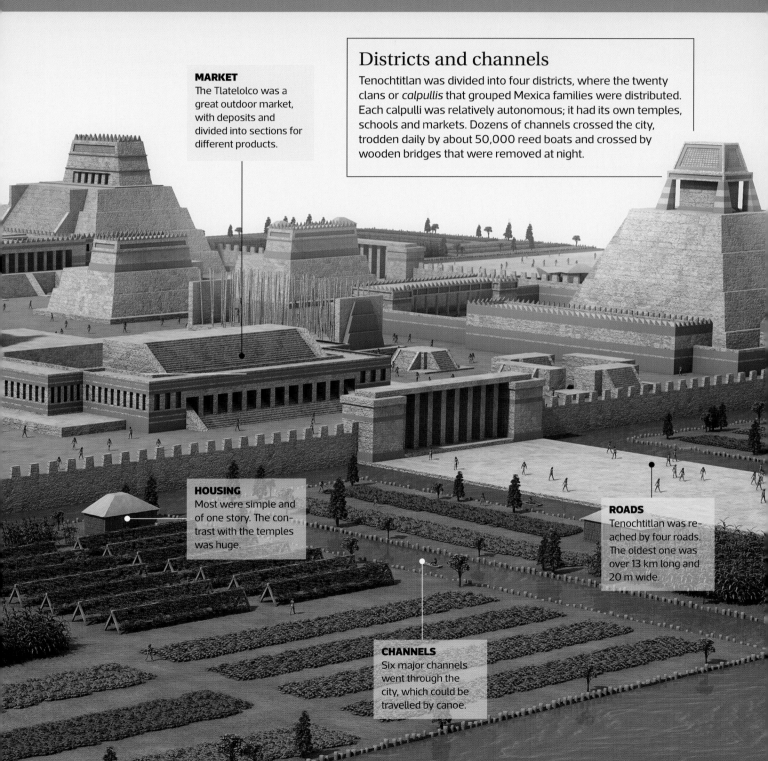

MARKET
The Tlatelolco was a great outdoor market, with deposits and divided into sections for different products.

Districts and channels

Tenochtitlan was divided into four districts, where the twenty clans or *calpullis* that grouped Mexica families were distributed. Each calpulli was relatively autonomous; it had its own temples, schools and markets. Dozens of channels crossed the city, trodden daily by about 50,000 reed boats and crossed by wooden bridges that were removed at night.

HOUSING
Most were simple and of one story. The contrast with the temples was huge.

ROADS
Tenochtitlan was reached by four roads. The oldest one was over 13 km long and 20 m wide.

CHANNELS
Six major channels went through the city, which could be travelled by canoe.

Inca cities

The Inca civilization born in Cuzco (Peru) created a great empire in the Andes between the fifteenth and sixteenth centuries. The Incas were skilled engineers, builders, and developed efficient irrigation engineering in agricultural terraces and they built cities, palaces and roads.

Machu Picchu, the Sacred City

Among the Inca buildings, the Machu Micchu stands out; it is a monumental and stepped hidden city in the mountains, with an amazing urban planning. Built in the mid fifteenth century, it was divided into two sectors, one for farming and an urban one. In the center of the urban sector, there was the great main Square. In turn, as all Inca cities, Machu Picchu had an "upper area" or *hanan* (sacred area), and a "lower area," called urin (residential area).

The stone work

Machu Picchu stands out for the high quality of its masonry work, the stone carving techniques and the perfect fit of walls. The procedure to give stones the desired shape was simple but time consuming

1 Extraction
Wooden wedges were inserted into cracks in the rocks to widen them.

2 Softening
Water was poured to swell the wood until the rock cracked.

3 Polishing
Percussion of stones was carried out to smooth them, and then they were polished with sand and water.

SEPARATION
A staircase, a wall and a pit, which in turn is a drain channel, separate the urban and agriculture sectors.

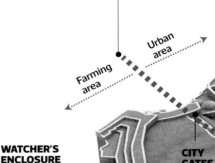

Farming area

Urban area

CEMETERY

FUNERARY ROCK

WATCHER'S ENCLOSURE

CITY GATES

FARMING TERRACES

EXTERIOR BARRACKS
Series of five buildings located at the bottom of the mountain, one on each level of the terraces. It is believed that they served to control one of the major roads into the city.

Imperial residence

Most researchers agree that Inca Pachacutec was the founder and first ruler of Tawantinsuyu (Inca empire), who ordered the construction of this citadel as a playground and shelter during the winter, located 118 km away from Cuzco and at about 1,200 km from Lima, the capital of Peru. The reason for its abandonment is unknown, as some houses are unfinished.

HIDDEN ENCLAVE
Machu Picchu was built between Huayna Picchu and Machu Picchu peaks in a strategic access hampered by two deep canyons and the gorges of the Urubamba River.

INTIHUATANA
It means "the stone where the sun is tied." Some thought it was a sundial. Other people believe that it served to indicate the position of the sun during the solstices or even that it was a sacrificial altar.

STONE QUARRIES

PARSONAGE

MAIN TEMPLE

TEMPLE OF THE THREE WINDOWS

MAIN SQUARE

SACRED ROCK

Hanan Urin

LA CASA DEL INCA
It was a royal residence. It had a private room, a bathroom and a green area as a garden. It follows that it belonged to royalty for its delicate construction.

TEMPLE OF THE SUN
Semicircular tower. Two of the windows are aligned with the sunrise during the summer and winter solstices.

GROUP OF MORTARS
Inside, there are two circular fountains, identified as mortars; therefore, this area is called the Industrial Area.

TEMPLE OF THE CONDOR
Ceremonial center. Named by an enigmatic representation on its base.

GROUP OF THE THREE GATES
Some call it the Quarter of *amautas or teachers*.

The Inca housing

The houses of the Inca farmers had a single rectangular floor for the whole family. When a couple was united in marriage, the community helped in the construction of new housing, and the state would give them a piece of land for support.

Practical and simple

The walls of the houses were built of rough stone and mud or adobe, and the floors were packed dirt. The houses almost completely lacked of household furnishings, they merely had the necessary utensils to prepare food. In cities where there was less space, some houses had two floors, with access to the upper floor and a rope ladder, sometimes made of wood.

CEILINGS
They had a gable design and were made of an overlay of straw or "ichu" grass, supported by an internal skeleton of sticks.

ROADS
The Incas developed a system of roads in forests and rough terrain. Usually, they followed a straight line of assembled rocks. On slopes, they built stone steps.

Community life

The daily life of Inca society developed within the *ayllu*, peasant communities united by family ties and that had common ancestors and inhabited the same territory. The Inca society was governed by two principles: reciprocity and redistribution. Reciprocity included the need for ongoing mutual aid; and the redistribution of food and supplies was the responsibility of the State.

Techniques and materials

The Incas had a good knowledge of stone work, even for stones of large sizes, and they polished their sides for a precise fit. The houses of the nobles had more carefully done finishes, especially for rock polishing.

They combined various sizes and shapes of stone, although rectangular ones predominated.

This is a characteristic combination of small pebbles that was called "swarm."

WORSHIP
Deeply religious, the Incas included small niches in walls to house the statue of their main deity.

FURNITURE
The Inca houses had no furniture. They slept on a blanket on the floor. There were also no chairs, so they ate on the floor.

AS A PERCH
They placed projections of wood or bone to hang clothes.

DOORS
Narrow and covered with a mat or wool curtain. They were the only means of ventilation, as the windows were rare and if there were placed, they were very small.

FIRE
Located in the center of the house, it was essential for cooking food and to temper the low temperatures of the Andean nights.

The Mongolian yurt

At the beginning of the second millennium, many nomadic peoples still used portable housing in their journeys. As from the Middle Ages, the Mongols, originating from the steppes of Central Asia, implemented circular campaign tents called *yurts*.

In constant motion

The Mongols roamed vast distances in adverse conditions, and needed tents that could easily be assembled and immediately lifted if circumstances required it. They protected them with a thick cover, they were easy to transport and were effective when enduring extreme temperature ranges in the region. Each family had a yurt, and visits between neighbors involved a rigorous protocol. Even, a person could be severely punished for merely entering the home of a superior without being duly announced.

SOIL
These homes were usually assembled directly on the ground, although in the case of wealthy families, they did it on wooden floors covered with carpets.

DOOR
There was only one wide gateway. It was enclosed by a frame of boards attached to the central body of the tent by means of ropes.

Family ties
Nearby yurts usually belonged to members of the same clan. The distribution was dictated by blood ties.

CURTAINS
Cloth or canvas that hung from the rafters, at certain distance from the walls. They separated the common area (center) from the private areas.

UPPER RING
Vent and light opening that bore the tension of the beams on which the ceiling was mounted.

Expansion
The Mongols were a series of nomadic tribes who moved in an agile way through large parts of Asia; therefore, they used the yurt. However, with the rise of their mighty leader, Genghis Khan, they managed to settle definitively and they established an empire that challenged even the ancient Chinese forces.

COATING
According to the season, the yurts were covered with layers of straw or coarse woollen fabrics secured with tightening ropes.

INSIDE
Yurts, very stark, just had a low table, carpets to rest and trunks with personal items and goods. The brazier, in the center, was essential for cooking and heating.

Tradition and evolution
To settle the yurt in the old fashioned way, first the walls were assembled and door frame was mounted; then the rafters and the center ring were placed, and, finally, the coating fabrics were hung. Originally, the yurt was only movable. At present, it can also be fixed, and while it retains the original shape, it is constructed with modern materials.

STORAGE
The animals they hunted and fruits they gathered were deposited inside the homes.

BEAMS
Wooden supports that converged in an upper central ring. The force was exerted concentrically, without using pillars inside the house.

WALLS
They were called *janas*. They were made of timber, which, in turn, served as the backbone of the housing.

The Chinese siheyuan

The Ming Dynasty (1368-1644) established its capital in Beijing and implemented a rigid urban layout following the precepts of harmony spread by Confucius. Privileged sectors were allowed to build large homes called siheyuan.

An intimate and secluded home

The siheyuan were projected on an axis to ensure symmetry and balance. A central courtyard was the most important area of the home and was surrounded by four side buildings oriented to the cardinal points. Privacy was a key value preserved behind the adjacent walls and gardens.

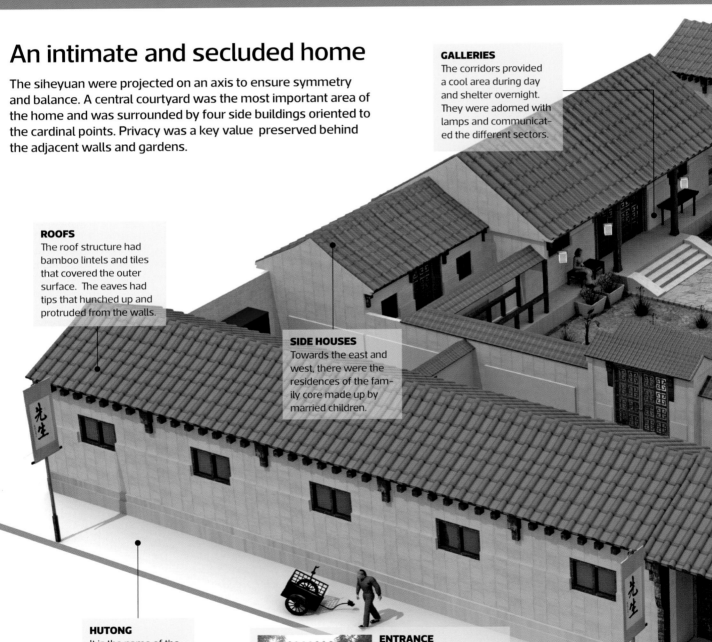

GALLERIES
The corridors provided a cool area during day and shelter overnight. They were adorned with lamps and communicated the different sectors.

ROOFS
The roof structure had bamboo lintels and tiles that covered the outer surface. The eaves had tips that hunched up and protruded from the walls.

SIDE HOUSES
Towards the east and west, there were the residences of the family core made up by married children.

HUTONG
It is the name of the straight and narrow lanes bordering the siheyuan.

ENTRANCE
The front door was painted with vermilion and decorated with a zoomorphic bronze knocker. Stone sculptures of lions used to be located on either side of the access stairway.

MAIN HOUSE
Located in the northern sector, it was used by the head of the family. Its eastern end is reserved for the first wife and the western end, for the concubines.

THE SIHEYUAN NOW
Today, many of these buildings are used as tea houses, restaurants or hotels that take advantage of the original architecture of the siheyuan.

GARDENS
They represented the harmony between man and nature. The lotus flower signifies purity emerging from the mud, and the willow, spiritual integrity.

先生

DISCRETION
A sheltered backyard communicated it with units assigned to unmarried daughters.

先生

FRONT YARD
Here, visitors awaited to be received. Workspaces and servants rooms were located it it.

The Hakka tulou

Another type of Chinese housing is the tulou, spread by the Hakka ethnic group in the mountain and rural regions of south-western Fujian. Erected since the twelfth century, they have a closed central precinct, either rectangular or circular, surrounded by units distributed between 3 and 5 stories. They used to house nearly a hundred families.

Classical China

The walled complex around big palatial buildings constituted the heart of traditional Chinese cities such as Nanjing and Kaifeng. This was also the case of the Forbidden City in Beijing, the world's largest palace complex.

The Forbidden City

The Forbidden City was the power hub of the Ming (1368-1644) and Qing (1644-1911) Dynasties for 500 years. It was built between 1406 and 1420, and 24 emperors lived there. It covers 720,000 m^2 and was conceived as core of the concentric sectors in which the Ming Dynasty divided Beijing: the outside (south of the city), for ceremonial purposes and dedicated to the people; the inside, for senior officials; and the center or Forbidden City (northern sector), for the emperor. Trespassing meant death.

ROOMS
On both sides of the North–South axis, over 9,000 halls and rooms of wood are symmetrically distributed.

GOLDEN WATER RIVER
It goes through the entrance square and five bridges cross it.

DEFENCES
The Forbidden City was surrounded by a pit with water that was 6 meters deep and 52 meters wide.

GATE OF HEAVENLY PEACE
Located on the south side, it is the main entrance to the complex.

Creator

In 1402, Yongle became the third emperor of the Ming Dynasty. Under his reign, China experienced a period of glory. He transferred the imperial capital of Nanjing to Beijing and ordered the creation of the Forbidden City.

THE CITY, TODAY

In 1911, a revolution overthrew the last imperial dynasty. Since then, the complex is a museum open to the public attracting seven million visitors each year.

WALLS
More than 8 feet high, they were thick as to resist the attacks of cannons.

THE THREE PAVILIONS
The Taihe, Zhonghe and Baohe palaces or Halls of Harmony were the most important buildings of the complex. They had ceremonial functions.

INTERNAL YARD
The northern zone was intended for the residence of the emperor, his family and his eunuchs and servants.

ELITE RESIDENCES
They housed the aristocracy. The roofs were made of yellow glazed tiles, which was the imperial color.

Location

The Forbidden City was built right in the middle of ancient Beijing, which was crossed by the Great Wall of China, fortification erected between the V and XVI centuries BC.

Forbidden City

Chinese Wall

The Renaissance city

A new city style emerged in Europe during the fifteenth century: the streets were straight and wider, whole neighborhoods were demolished for cars and people to circulate easily and main roads connecting plazas, palaces and cathedrals were opened.

Florence, a Renaissance jewel

The Italian city of Florence became the epicenter of the renewal of art and ideas that marked the Renaissance. Fruit of a Roman and medieval heritage, the city was enlarged and remodelled with the intention of improving its antiquated structure. Its power lay in banking and finances and it was usual for buildings, monuments and sculptures to be inaugurated under the new Renaissance aesthetics. On its streets walked prominent figures of the time, such as Leonardo da Vinci, Michelangelo and Machiavelli.

PIAZZA DELLA SIGNORIA
The Florentine Republic was born in this closed square, where the hot topics of local politics were discussed (115-1532). As the seat of civil power, it was the site where public executions were made.

HOUSING
The poorest people lived in small houses, made of wood and mortar. The middle classes lived in brick buildings and the nobility and high bourgeoisie in palaces.

TRIBUNALE DELLA MERCANZIA
With a Romanesque style, the Court was where the differences between the artisans were settled.

The heart of the city
The Arno River crosses the city. The main buildings are located around Ponte Vecchio, one of the bridges that crosses said river.

Piazza del Duomo

Piazza della Signoria

Palazzo Pitti

Medieval heritage

The new Renaissance style had to live in the ancient cities jointly with medieval elements like the tangle of streets and palaces with towers of Gothic style, such as the Palazzo Vecchio.

INTERIORS
The Hall of Five Hundred in the Palazzo Vecchio is one of the exponents of Renaissance interiors that house medieval buildings. It was decorated by Vasari.

PALAZZO VECCHIO
Seat of the city government, it was built in 1299-1314 by Arnolfo di Cambio. Its Gothic tower, known as Tower of Arnolfo, is one of the emblems of the city.

LOGGIA DEI LANZI
Portico of the fourteenth century turned into a kind of open air museum in the sixteenth century, with a gallery of statues.

FONTANA DEL NETTUNO
The Fountain of Neptune, also called Il Biancone, was created by Bartolomeo Ammannati. It was the first public fountain in Florence; Neptune referred to its sea power.

STATUE OF DAVID
The work of Michelangelo is 4 m high. To take it to the square, arches were demolished. It took 5 days.

CRAFTSMEN AND TRADERS
Their houses used to have a vaulted room that faced the street where the workshop or store was located for retail sale of raw materials or manufactured products.

Renaissance urban house

The various artistic movements that developed during the Renaissance sought to recover the appearance and harmony of ancient Greece and Rome; thus, straight lines, columns and domes were used again. It was a time of palaces and large houses.

A comprehensive home

Dwellings acquired enormous significance and became the center of social life. The wealthiest sectors, such as large traders, built palaces and mansions following the dictates of the new artistic trends. These multi-storey homes housed the most intimate family unit, other relatives and servants. Many also included work areas, commercial stores and offices.

HIGH WINDOWS
They lit and aired the central rooms. Glass windows were rare and were only found in luxurious mansions.

WOOD AND STONE
They were the basic materials used in the construction of homes.

Business

The expansion of interregional trade caused businesses to become incorporated into everyday life and within the same household. Therefore, family businesses usually operated on the ground floor of Renaissance houses, carried out in stores that faced the street and remained open throughout the day.

Renaissance Pharmacy. Fresco of Castle Issogne, Italy, XV century.

COMBINED STYLES
The straight-line architecture and high buildings fused with arches typical of classicism. Arched doors for access were common at the time.

KITCHEN
It used to be located on the top floor. It was far from the living room and the bedroom, to prevent odors and noise.

Residences in the field

Wealthier families had luxurious country residences. Villa Capra, located on the outskirts of the city of Vicenza, Italy, dates from 1566. This work of Italian Andrea Palladio is one of the best examples of this type of construction.

LIVING ROOM
It was the largest room in the house. In it, guests were received and major family events, such as weddings, were held.

LIGHTING
The environments had a diffuse illumination since, generally, wax paper was used to cover hollow spaces.

COURTYARD
Heart of the house, it was an innovation proper of the Renaissance. The main rooms overlooked this internal and open space to allow certain intimacy.

COLONNADE
Inspired by the palaces and temples of ancient Greece and Rome.

MASTER BEDROOM
It was not only used to rest. It was also the meeting point of the family, that is to say, the private space for parents and children.

The Baroque city

Exuberance and splendor are reflected in Baroque urbanism. Great royal squares and wide avenues for movement of carriages characterized cities like Rome, Madrid and Vienna in the seventeenth and eighteenth centuries. Also Paris, with its boulevards and palatial buildings.

Monumental Paris

Under the reign of Henry IV (1589-1610), Paris began a transformation that would turn it into a symbol of the royal power and prestige of the new dynasty which ruled France. His successor Louis XIII (1610-1643) and Louis XIV (1643-1715) would continue these reforms under the influence of the baroque. New districts like Marais, Temple, Louvre-Tuileries, Saint Germain and Saint Louis were created, and the palaces of the Louvre and the Tuileries were extended. The urban layout was configured based on cross streets: two main roads crossing a square and parallel pathways that created other squares. In addition, wide boulevards were opened.

TUILERIES PALACE
Catherine de Medici, wife of Henry IV, commissioned its construction in 1564 and it was remodelled and enlarged by Louis XIV. A fire destroyed it in 1871.

ORDER AND SYMMETRY
With Louis XIV, the parks acquired the "à la française" garden style: geometry and symmetry, nature in order.

The incidence of Richelieu

Chief minister of Louis XIII from 1624 to 1642, Cardinal Richelieu wanted Paris to reflect its actual glory. He commissioned architect Jacques Lemercier the construction of the Royal Palace and a residency in Indre-et-Loire (image).

LOUIS XIV, THE INNOVATOR

Louis XIV ordered the creation of the first boulevard in 1670. It ran from the Porte Saint-Denis to the Bastille. The boulevards would be continued after 1870 by Haussman.

PONT ROYAL

It crosses the River Seine, and was completed in 1689 by order of Louis XIV. It is the third oldest bridge in Paris.

Continued reforms

In 1870, the prefect Baron Georges-Eugène Haussmann was commissioned to reform Paris. He replaced narrow streets with wide boulevards arranged radially, from the Arc de Triomphe.

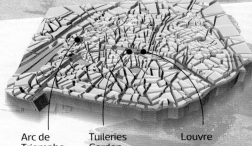

Arc de Triomphe   Tuileries Garden   Louvre

The evolution of the garden

Since the first gardens were designed in Ancient Times, the function and aesthetics of these green spaces have evolved throughout history, constituting a true reflection of different cultures and eras in which they were conceived.

The value of green spaces

The first gardens emerged in ancient Mesopotamia and Egypt and, in the Middle Ages, they acquired a symbolic value in Eastern and Muslim cultures in which the art of gardening was directly related to the concept of harmony between man and nature. In the West, the gardens were restricted to the upper classes for centuries and they were not integrated into urban homes until the late nineteenth century.

Japanese minkas

The minka or cottage housing is a type of dwelling of Japanese origin dating from the Kofun Period, around the third century. The most important area of this residence was a back room directly integrated with the garden, which constituted a private area shared in family.

Egyptian oasis

The first gardens on record were located in Egypt. The exotic plants and flowers, especially lotus, received particular care given the adverse conditions of dessert weather.

DISTRIBUTION
Gardens used to be surrounded by trees, which provided shadow, and they had a central pond.

ROCKS
Even if stone was not used in the construction of the house, it was an important element of garden décor.

PONDS
Several natural springs or artificial ponds could be part of the garden. The water symbolized harmony with nature.

Chronology
The evolution of gardens throughout history is detailed below.

2000 BC – 31 BC	Century I BC – Century III AD	Century III	Middle Ages – Century X
Egypt The first gardens were designed by order of Pharaohs to decorate temples, palaces and burial vaults.	**Rome** Both urban domus and rural villas had well-kept and landscaped gardens with hedges and fountains.	**Japan** The Japanese gardens appeared as a new interpretation on the millenarian parameters of the Chinese Feng Shui.	**Muslim culture** For such culture, a garden is the earthly expression of Paradise. Therefore, they put great emphasis on its design and decoration.

SPECIES
Various species of flowers, herbs and fruit trees abounded.

REDUCED GARDENS
City houses have small gardens, mainly a lawn area and at least one tree in each façade.

Arab style

The Islamic garden is designed as a closed space that seeks intimacy and delighting the senses. When the dimensions allow it, courtyards and pergolas are attached to outdoor areas.

Industrial era

With industrialization, urban population increased and so did the noise and dirt. In more affluent neighborhoods, green spaces –though still small– were integrated to the houses, while the richer sectors chose to move to outlying areas where large parks and private gardens were a real privilege.

TILES
They were adorned with ceramic tiles of bright colors on the floor and on benches.

WATER
Present in fountains and channels, it was a key element of the garden composition.

The baroque gardens

In Europe, during the seventeenth century a type of garden was developed and designed to show the grandeur of the absolutist reigns. The French garden with lawns and flower beds, and artificial constructions such as caves, theaters, or islands, is the paradigm of this type of garden.

Gardens of Versailles (France), designed by André Le Nôtre.

XV – XVI Centuries	XVII Century	XVIII Century	XIX – XX Centuries
Renaissance Roman customs are recovered. Gardens appear around great palaces with sculpted shrubs.	**Baroque** Lush gardens with geometric designs, labyrinthine paths, sculptures, fountains and a great variety of plants and flowers.	**English landscapes** In rejecting the baroque, English landscape designers conceived parks to respect the natural landforms, such as hills.	**Urban gardens** As from the last decades of the nineteenth century in Western European cities, parks and gardens have been conceived as part of urban design.

Contemporary Age

Chapter 3

Neoclassicism permeated large cities of the eighteenth century and embellished them with elegant palaces, cathedrals and theaters. But the Industrial Revolution that began in the late eighteenth century in Great Britain meant a total transformation of the urban landscape in Europe. As cities were filled with factories, working class neighborhoods proliferated where workers lived in appalling and overcrowded conditions while the enriched bourgeoisie occupied residential neighborhoods with luxury homes. The arrival of the railroad and the improved communications brought a steady stream of travellers to the cities, which grew at an overwhelming pace. New materials such as concrete and steel, and the invention of the elevator, allowed buildings to grow tall. Soon there were skyscrapers and cities with over one million inhabitants. In the late twentieth century, a new phenomenon, the megacities, which are urban clusters that can reach 20 million inhabitants, raised new urban challenges and the concern for achieving sustainable cities and homes, taking advantage of the possibilities offered by new technologies.

The Neoclassical city

In the eighteenth century, the great cities were transformed according to the premises of Neoclassicism, inspired by classical antiquity. The main streets were widened, along with the appearance of groves, walk paths, large squares and monumental buildings.

St. Petersburg

In 1703, Tsar Peter the Great began the construction of St. Petersburg adopting the neoclassical style that prevailed in Western Europe. Capital of the Russian empire from 1712 to 1917, it grew under successive tsars who shaped the luxury and grandeur of the royal court.

THE ADMIRALTY
Architectural center of St. Petersburg, three main streets are born from it.

CATHEDRAL OF ST. ISAAC
With almost 102 m of height, it is the highest cathedral in Russia. 43 different kinds of mineral and marble from different countries were used in its decoration.

Rivers and canals

The layout of St. Petersburg is crossed by 93 rivers and canals. The communication ways include over three hundred bridges.

Cathedral of St. Isaac

Winter Palace

Neva River

Greatness, Russian style

When Peter the Great died in 1725, the city was booming, but his successors neglected it. It was Elizabeth, crowned in 1742, who would boost its rebirth. Under her reign, the city went on to become a splendid capital of 150,000 inhabitants. Its palaces were the most lavish of Europe and its academies and theaters attracted intellectuals and artists from the West.

THE VERSAILLES OF THE TSARS
Tsarskoe Selo is the most dazzling city palace. Supreme symbol of the power of the Tsars.

WINTER PALACE
Official residence of the Tsars, erected to display their greatness. Its taking by the Bolsheviks in 1917 marks the beginning of the Russian Revolution.

BRIDGES
The city has 342 bridges; the main ones are movable, such as the Lomonosov.

NEVSKY AVENUE
4 km long, it is the main street. The oldest section goes from the Palace Square to the Uprising Square.

Catherine the Great

She reigned from 1762 to 1796 and left great works in the city: she built the Hermitage Theater, the Alexander Institute and new buildings of the Academy of Sciences and the Imperial Academy of Arts.

Industrial cities

With the Industrial Revolution, in the eighteenth and nineteenth centuries, the growth of cities accelerated, often beyond their capacity. Factories, workshops and warehouses filled the cities and the population grew quickly.

Manchester

The English city of Manchester was the first to industrialize. Between 1760 and 1830 its population multiplied tenfold (from 17,000 to 180,000 inhabitants) and the city grew at the same pace. Along with factories, working class neighborhoods proliferated and gave the city infrastructure to facilitate the transit of goods. An entire city based on its industry.

POLLUTION
The smoke from factories, as well as the waste thrown into the river or accumulated on the street, vitiated the atmosphere.

Infrastructure for industry

In 1761, the Manchester Bridgewater Canal, considered the first of England, was inaugurated to transport coal to the industrial areas of Manchester. It triggered the so-called "channel fever" which lasted until the 1830s, when the massive introduction of the railroad offered a faster and cheaper way to transport goods and passengers. In 1830, the railway line linking Manchester with Liverpool became operational and, in 1844, Victoria Station opened.

Victoria Station

River Irwell   Bridgewater Canal   Rochdale Canal

HOUSING
The houses of the working class neighborhoods were built near the factories and lacked a planned layout.

INLAND WATERWAY RESOURCE
The channelling of the River Irwell allowed further navigability and enhanced trade flows.

The triumph of engineering

During the Industrial Revolution, the role of architecture in the planning and construction of cities was questioned for the first time in centuries. Technological advances, which adapted more to the skills of engineers than to architects' art, accounted for its mechanization and engineering works prevailed on architecture.

A REVOLUTIONARY
Engineer Isambard Kingdom Brunel (1806-1859) built bridges, ports, railways (was the creator of the British Great Western Railway line) and ocean liners with innovative techniques.

WITHOUT UTILITIES
The working class neighborhoods lacked public services of sewerage or drinking water supply.

STORES
In these huge sheds, dispersed between factories, the raw products were kept: cotton, tobacco, coal, etc.

LOW LIGHT
The streets were poorly lit. There were a few oil lamps per block which gave a dim light.

COTTON CITY
Most of the industry in Manchester was made up of cotton mills imported from the United States at a cheap cost. This gave the *Cottonopolis* nickname to the city.

PROLETARIANIZATION
Workers stopped having occupations to become a cog in the production chain.

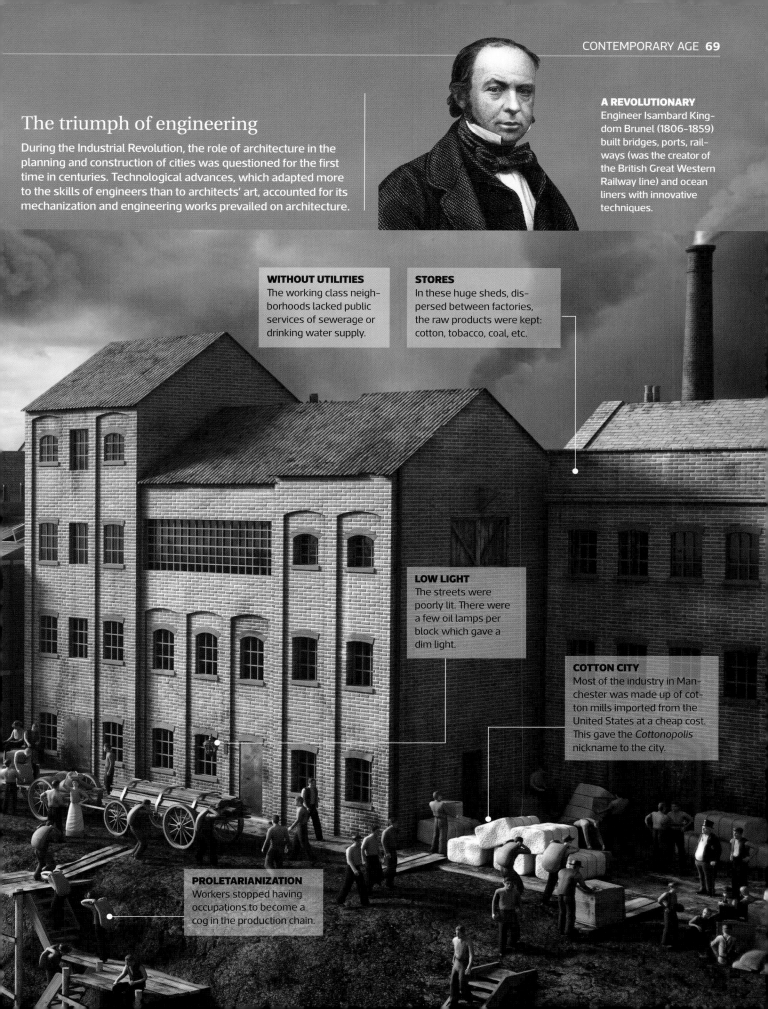

House of the working class

With industrialization there was a large influx to the city of labor for factories, which resulted in the construction of large working class neighborhoods that were overcrowded and where workers lived in appalling conditions.

Overcrowded and unsanitary

The neighborhoods of workers' housing in industrial cities were poor, noisy and overcrowded. Houses were arranged in rows, near the factories where adults and children worked exhausting hours. These neighborhoods were prone to overcrowding and unsanitary conditions where several families, which usually had many children, shared small spaces.

ATTIC
It was small and not all houses had it. Sometimes it was rented to single workers.

SHARED BATHROOMS
They were in a narrow room located next to the row of houses. Several families used one: typically, a block of 40 houses could count with only six bathrooms.

BEDROOM
Spouses and children often shared a room on top as bedroom.

HOMELESS CHILDREN
It was not considered negative for children to work in factories, mines or have other occupations such as shoeshiner. They could have 16-hour workdays and received less pay than adults. There were also many orphans engaged in begging, which was considered a crime.

GROUND FLOOR
Only one room used to work as kitchen, dining and living room.

In the field

During the industrial era, the houses of the rural sectors were also humble though, unlike urban houses, their inhabitants did not suffer overcrowding. They families were equally numerous and shared all daily tasks.

SPACES
The field houses could have stables, areas of manual labor and farming.

WALLS AND CEILING
The walls were thin and made of red bricks, and the noises from neighboring apartments could easily be heard. The ceilings were of black or blue slate.

LAYOUT
The row-houses allowed maximizing space. There could be up to three rows of houses together. Only the first one of them had small backyards.

DRINKING WATER
In the beginning, the pipe system did not reach the houses of working-class neighborhoods. Water was obtained from public fountains.

BASEMENTSS
They were rooms of cheap rent that usually were very wet and dark. Sometimes they could be occupied by more than one family.

The cottages

They were built by English entrepreneurs of the nineteenth century in the peripheral areas of large cities as a solution to the housing need of working classes at the beginning of the industrialization. These sets of houses soon became widespread in Europe and elsewhere.

A new urban landscape

During the second half of the nineteenth century, economic activity in cities increased with the improvement of communications. The streets were filled with travellers, noise and traffic, and the life quality of the people improved significantly.

Liverpool and Lime Street

Where the railroad appeared, the landscape changed. Next to each new station, a hotel was usually built for travellers and the shops and cafes multiplied. In the English city of Liverpool, which during the late nineteenth century was considered the second city of the Empire and which became richer than London, Lime Street was the symbol of said era of urban transformations.

HOTEL
The Great North Western Hotel was built to house travellers arriving at the train station. It opened its doors in 1879.

LIME STREET
It opened in 1790 and was located at the edge of the old town. It owed its name to the presence of *lime* kilns.

PUBS
As more people walked along Lime Street, pubs like The Crown (it was the first one, in 1859) and The Vines were opened.

ST. GEORGE'S HALL
Opposite to the station and the hotel, there was the square for the large public building of St. George's Hall, where courts functioned.

Communications, axis of economic activity

The station and the port were the two axes structuring the economic life of the city of Liverpool. In the nineteenth century, 40% of world seaborne trade went through its docks, the train linked it to Manchester and its customs office was the largest contributor to the British treasury.

St. George's Hall

Lime Street

Lime Station

Albert Dock

Pioneer city

Its lively port, the first in the world to have a commercial dry dock -the Thomas Steer Dock, in 1715-, allowed the city of Liverpool to be a pioneer in several fields as reflected in both the port and the railway line, which produced its explosive urban growth.

TRAIN
In 1830, Liverpool and Manchester were the first cities linked by a railway line.

STATION
Its construction started in 1833 and it officially opened in 1836, completely changing the appearance of the street, which became noisier and busier.

TRAFFIC
Private cars, stage-coaches for passengers (a kind of bus pulled by horses) circulated in Lime Street.

Bourgeois house

By the end of the nineteenth century, a powerful bourgeoisie had consolidated in the main European cities. Their houses, with several storeys, evidenced the economic growth of that time and showed the high social level reached by certain bourgeois sectors.

Distribution of the house

The owners lived on the first floor, which was the most accessible, bright and airy. Its spacious apartments and had luxurious and decorated rooms. The second and third floors, more modest, were rented to close people. The basement and the attic, confined and uncomfortable spaces, were reserved for the servants and humble people. This uneven distribution of the rooms reflected the order and logic governing the organization of the capitalist society.

MAIN HALL
It was the favorite place of bourgeois families. It was decorated with special attention to arouse the admiration of the guests.

FLOOR OF THE OWNER
The first floor was reserved for the building owner and his family. The rooms were spacious and well distributed. They were bright and easily accessible.

Modern house

The English architect Philip Webb built the "Red House" in South East London in 1859, commissioned by Wiiliam Morris. Emblem of the nascent modern house, it is distinguished for being made of red brick, without any kind of plaster.

HALL AND STAIRCASE
The hall used to be decorated with ornaments, carved furniture, paintings and sculptures. Also, the main staircase linking all floors of the house was placed in the hall.

KITCHEN
The cooking of meals was carried out in an exclusive room for this purpose. Coal was incorporated as fuel for kitchen appliances.

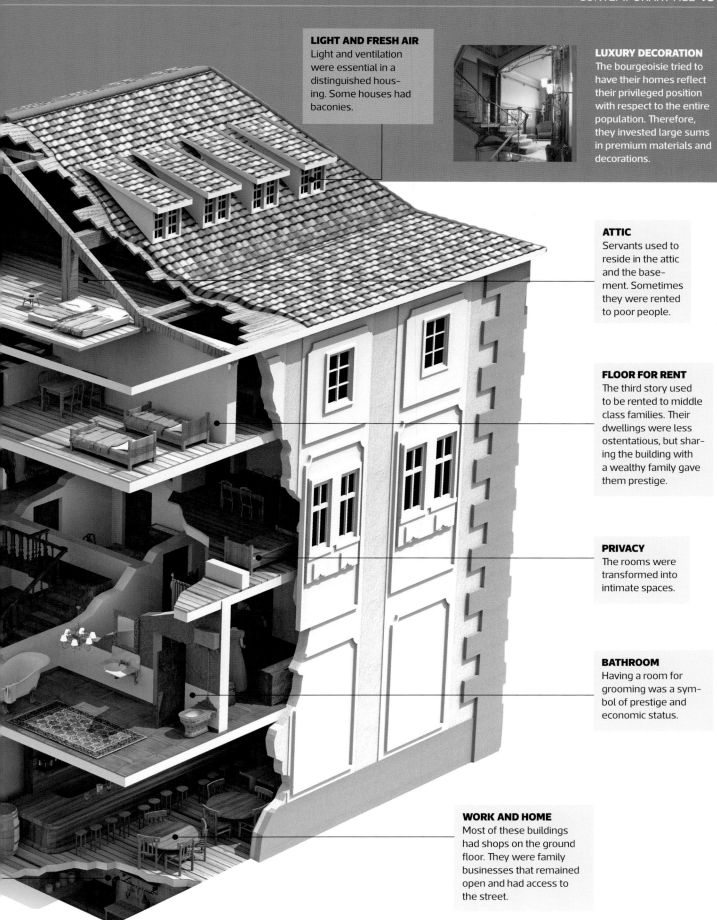

LIGHT AND FRESH AIR
Light and ventilation were essential in a distinguished housing. Some houses had baconies.

LUXURY DECORATION
The bourgeoisie tried to have their homes reflect their privileged position with respect to the entire population. Therefore, they invested large sums in premium materials and decorations.

ATTIC
Servants used to reside in the attic and the basement. Sometimes they were rented to poor people.

FLOOR FOR RENT
The third story used to be rented to middle class families. Their dwellings were less ostentatious, but sharing the building with a wealthy family gave them prestige.

PRIVACY
The rooms were transformed into intimate spaces.

BATHROOM
Having a room for grooming was a symbol of prestige and economic status.

WORK AND HOME
Most of these buildings had shops on the ground floor. They were family businesses that remained open and had access to the street.

Large metropolises

Between the late nineteenth and early twentieth century, new cities emerged that were filled with skyscrapers and became metropolises, cities with over one million inhabitants erected in the economic, political and cultural center of a region or country.

New York, the city of skyscrapers

The advances in iron and reinforced concrete, as well as the emergence of the electric lift, coupled with increasingly high land prices, led to build ever taller buildings. At the rhythm of skyscrapers delineating a new horizon, Unite States saw the birth of the great cities, of which New York is considered the quintessence.

POPULATION
In 1900, nearly 3.5 million people lived in New York. Today it is the most populous city in the country, with more than 8 million inhabitants.

GE BUILDING
Thus named for belonging to General Electric, this Art Deco 259-meter high skyscraper stands in the middle of Rockefeller Center.

RIVERS AND BRIDGES
32% of the surface of the County of New York is water. In total, 75 bridges link the five boroughs of the city.

Manhattan

The city area is 780 km², divided into five boroughs: Manhattan, Bronx, Brooklyn, Queens and Staten Island. Manhattan is the heart of New York, where the main icons of the city are located.

Rockefeller Center

Chrysler Building

Empire State Building

Brooklyn Bridge

New York transforms itself

Between 1854 and 1934, New York became a great metropolis. During this period, it had its first telephone company (1878), electric lighting (1882), the Brooklyn Bridge; the Statue of Liberty (1886), the Natural History and Metropolitan museums, the underground system (1904) and the largest station in the world (Grand Central Station) (1913).

TRAFFIC LIGHTS
The first three-light traffic lights were installed in New York's Fifth Avenue in 1920. Two years later, they were operating automatically throughout Manhattan.

CHRYSLER BUILDING
Art Deco building inaugurated in 1930 that, with its 319-meters of height, was the tallest building in the city until the Empire State Building surpassed it in 1931.

SKYSCRAPERS
New York has about 4,490 skyscrapers. Steel and concrete were the construction materials used. Some of them were erected in record time, such as the Empire State, built in 410 days.

ROCKEFELLER CENTER
Between 1930 and 1939, the Rockefeller family built a complex of 14 commercial buildings in downtown Manhattan.

RAPID GROWTH
Most of the buildings in Manhattan are less than a hundred years old. The growth of cities in the last century was dizzying.

The apartment building

After World War II, new requirements arose for the cities which, along with the emergence of new materials, led to the birth of new architectural experiences. One was the construction of large apartment buildings.

Concrete and steel

The need to combine different factors, such as the appearance of concrete, the industrial production of steel and the success of elevators allowed the proliferation structures rising ever-higher. In the first decades of the twentieth century, skyscrapers for offices and commercial activities proliferated, which were soon followed by high compartmented buildings.

Arrival of the elevator

By mid 19th century, the elevators to transport people were invented. The toothed-belt pulley system granted better safety and soon they became an essential element for the proliferation of high apartment buildings.

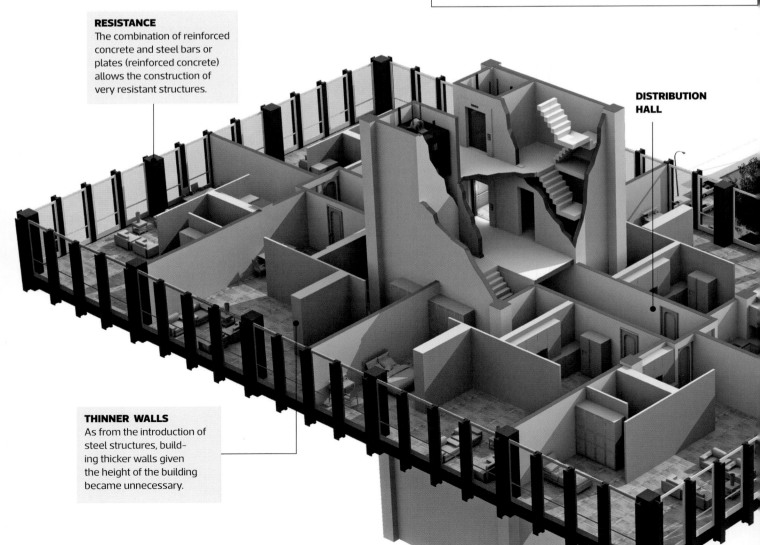

RESISTANCE
The combination of reinforced concrete and steel bars or plates (reinforced concrete) allows the construction of very resistant structures.

DISTRIBUTION HALL

THINNER WALLS
As from the introduction of steel structures, building thicker walls given the height of the building became unnecessary.

LAKE SHORE DRIVE
These twin towers, designed by Ludwig Mies van der Rohe in 1949 in Chicago, are an example of the new architecture of steel and glass.

EXTERNAL GLASS
The outer walls have no support-ing function. Thus, they can be made of various types of materials, such as glass.

FOUNDATION
The foundation, part of the build-ing that distributes the weight of the structure on the ground, can be deep or shallow, depending on the terrain features and the size of the building.

Rationalist house

In the early twentieth century, the rationalist style of architecture spread throughout Europe. It applies the dynamic conception of spaces, the use of simple geometrical shapes and the direct relation between shape and function of spaces.

Villa Savoye. Work of Charles Le Corbusier, one of the leading exponents of architectural rationalism.

Megacities

Since the last decades of the twentieth century, some cities have grown at a dizzying pace together with surrounding conurbations, giving rise to large urban centers and megacities with more than 10 million inhabitants.

Sao Paulo

Born in 1554 as a small village, the Brazilian city of Sao Paulo grew first at the rate of the sugar industry and then at that of the coffee industry along the nineteenth and early twentieth centuries. Now, more than 20 million people live in its metropolitan area (eleven million in the city); it is the largest urban center in South America, and one of the most important business centers of Latin America.

URBAN RIVERS
The Tietê River and its tributary, the Pinheiros, ran across the city of Sao Paulo. Its waters present high levels of contamination.

HEIGHT
With 5,677 buildings over 35 m high, it is the third city in the world with the greatest number of tall buildings.

ROAD SYSTEM
The city of Sao Paulo has the largest highway network in Latin America.

VEHICLE FLEET
The city has over seven million vehicles, and the metropolitan area, ten million.

Bridge area

With 1968 km² of urban area, the city is divided into 31 sub-municipalities, each with 10 districts. The area of the Octavio Frias de Oliveira Bridge is known as Brooklin.

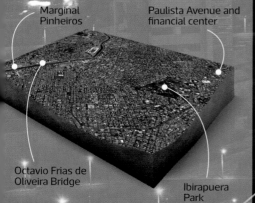

Marginal Pinheiros

Paulista Avenue and financial center

Octavio Frias de Oliveira Bridge

Ibirapuera Park

Other megacities

Among today's great megacities, there are Tokyo (Japan), Shanghai (China), Jakarta (Indonesia), Seoul (South Korea), Delhi (India), Karachi (Pakistan), Mumbai (India), Manila (Philippines), Mexico City (Mexico) and New York. They are all urban areas of more than 20 million inhabitants.

TRAFFIC CHAOS
In large cities like Tokyo, it is increasingly complex to manage population and vehicle fleet growth.

CITIES IN MOTION
It is home to 90,000 daily events of, inter alia, art, business and fashion. It has great night-life, the most dynamic in South America.

OCTAVIO FRIAS DE OLIVEIRA BRIDGE
Inaugurated in 2003, it crosses the Pinheiros River. Its unique design has made it a symbol of the city.

From city to megacity

In the early twentieth century, Sao Paulo had about 200,000 inhabitants. By the 1940s, the population began recording a continuous growth that would reach the present day.

1950
2,000,000 inhabitants

Municipality

Metropolitan area

1975
6,000,000 inhabitants

1995
9,800,000 inhabitants

Underground urbanism

With cities around the world being increasingly congested, it became necessary to seize underground space so as to accommodate infrastructures to sustain the large metropolises. Today, large cities grow downwards.

An underground world

The development of underground urbanism has emerged as a very effective yet sustainable option for urban development and renewal. In 1863, in London, the first subway system in the world was opened, and the idea was almost immediately adopted by other large cities. Today, the use of tunnels is not restricted to the subway; it is also feasible for utilities, highways, parking lots, pedestrian traffic, offices and even art spaces.

Minimising the impact

It is proved that megacities and large cities are the systems that exert the greatest impact on the planet. Underground planning helps to minimize this impact by building road alternatives that signify a relief to traffic congestion.

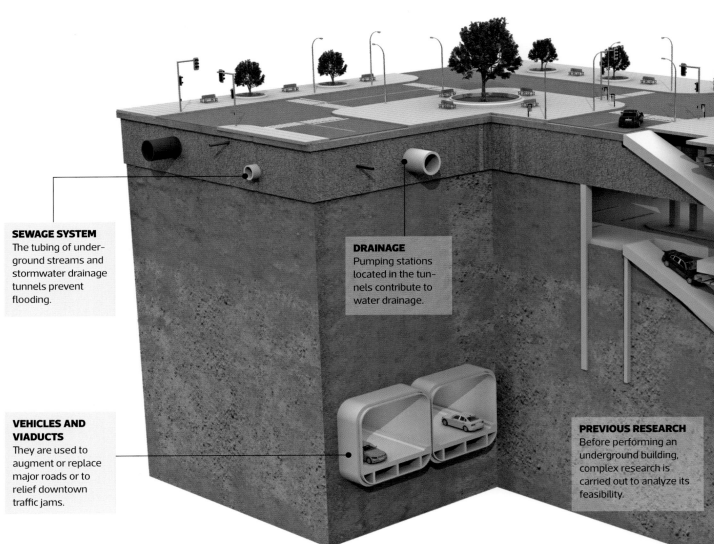

SEWAGE SYSTEM
The tubing of underground streams and stormwater drainage tunnels prevent flooding.

DRAINAGE
Pumping stations located in the tunnels contribute to water drainage.

VEHICLES AND VIADUCTS
They are used to augment or replace major roads or to relief downtown traffic jams.

PREVIOUS RESEARCH
Before performing an underground building, complex research is carried out to analyze its feasibility.

Montreal's Underground City

In the 1960s, the urban planner Vincent Ponte raised the idea of developing an underground city in Montreal, Canada, by interconnecting underground complexes through tunnels. Today, RÉSO in Montreal is one of the largest underground gallery networks of the world that connects metro stations, offices, hotels, shopping centers, museums and universities.

MORE THAN TUNNELS
The RÉSO has 190 points of entry and 32 km of tunnels with shops, restaurants and public buildings.

PARKING LOTS
The rising price of the land makes it cheaper to build underground parking lots.

The London Tube

The London underground system (a.k.a. the "Tube") is the oldest one in the world and it was the first to use electric trains. With 270 stations and 402 km of railways, it is one of the largest in the world, and it has one of the most imitated designs. More than four million passengers use the London tube every day.

Just tunnels
Unlike other metro systems, London's system is mostly tubed, instead of being built on covered trenches.

Picadilly Circus
This station is near Soho and the theater district.

Restructuring cities

By the late twentieth century, governments, urban planners and architects became aware of the need to curb urban degradation and to prioritize the quality of life of its inhabitants. Berlin, Antwerp, Lyon and Barcelona are examples of cities that recycled themselves.

Barcelona

The Catalan capital, which in 1860 had been reformed as from the extension plan, or Eixample, was renewed again between 1986 and 1992 for the celebration of the Olympic Games. The reform was carried out through interventions in specific areas in order to cause an improvement for the entire city and its inhabitants.

THE EIXAMPLE
Conceived by Ildefons Cerdá in 1860, it was built after the demolition of the medieval walls. It is located between the original core and ancient towns, now annexed.

THE RAVAL
The old neighbor-hood of el Raval is located o the left of La Rambla, which has been the subject of a major renova-tion for two decades.

LA RAMBLA
Since the fifteenth century, this promenade became the center of the city. It houses the Gran Teatro del Liceo and various bourgeois palaces.

Renovation of historic centers

One of the challenges of the large European cities is undertaking the renovation of historic neighborhoods that have deteriorated without destroying their essence. The Raval district of Barcelona is an example of this type of intervention, undertaken during the late 90s, by means of which new public spaces were opened, old buildings were reused and new cultural facilities were created.

RAMBLA OF THE RAVAL
Built in the heart of the neighborhood, it implied the demolition of five blocks of houses. It was inaugurated in 2000.

GOTHIC QUARTER
Historical center. In the nineteenth century, old buildings were recycled and parish cemeteries were turned into parks.

SAGRADA FAMILIA
(Expiatory Church of the Holy Family). Work by Antoni Gaudí. It is the epitome of modernist architecture in the city and one of its most iconic landmarks.

TECHNOLOGY DISTRICT
It is called 22@. It covers 200 ha and was opened in 2000. The Agbar Tower was designed by Jean Nouvel, opened in 2005 and marks the entry to the district.

Heritage and modernization

Barcelona is divided into 10 districts. The Ciutat Vella ("Old City") includes the Gothic Quarter and the historic center of the city, while the construction of the Olympic Village (with the recovery of the seafront) and the transformation of Montjuic (where most of the Olympic facilities were placed) are the two great urban interventions of the pre-Olympic period.

Eixample

Gothic Quarter

Montjuic

Olympic Village

The futuristic urbanism

The twenty-first century urbanism seeks answers to the growth of the world population by designing "future cities" that are based on three pillars: vertical construction, eco-efficiency and intelligence. Dubai, in the Persian Gulf, is an emblematic case.

Sci-Fi

Although the growth of Dubai in the UAE began in the 60s and 70s of the hand in hand with oil exports, as from the late 90's the city has experienced an architectural boom that filled it with skyscrapers and the most surprising buildings. It has more than 60 buildings over 200 meters high, the most luxurious hotel and the world's largest indoor ski slope, hundreds of artificial islands... all with the aim of attracting investors and tourists.

BURJ KHALIFA
Also known as Burj Dubai, it was opened in 2010; it is 828 meters high and has 900 apartments, as well as restaurants and offices.

The old and new Dubai

The Dubai Creek divides the city in two historic districts, Deira and Bur Dubai, while the financial district and the Jumeirah coastal area represent the new urbanism of the city.

World Islands
Jumeirah
Financial District
Deira
Sheikh Zayed Avenue
Bur Dubai
Dubai Creek

SHEIKH ZAYED AVENUE
It is the portion of the National E-11 highway that runs through the city along the coast. It has 6 lanes in each direction and it is flanked by towers and luxury hotels.

ARTIFICIAL LAKE
With 12 ha, it is the largest of its kind, which also has the longest fountain of the world.

Gigantism and pharaonic projects

The excessive focus on gigantism has made Dubai a "Sci-Fi city," which is dominated by artificiality, lack of cohesion, rapid growth and poor relationship with the environment. Among the pharaonic projects, there are the artificial island complexes called Palm Islands and The World, a 300-island archipelago that makes up the world map.

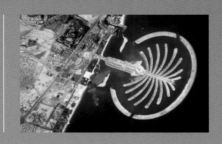

PALM JUMEIRAH
It is one of three artificial islands in the Palm Islands complex. It is shaped like a palm tree and it counts with 60 hotels and 5,000 villas.

Downtown Burj Khalifa

This complex extends over 2 km parallel to the Sheikh Zayed Avenue and it houses the Burj Khalifa, the tallest skyscraper in the world, and other buildings competing in eccentricity. The construction of this complex required an investment in excess of USD 20,000 million.

EMIRATES TOWERS
One of them is 355 m high and has offices and a convention center; the other one has a height of 309 m and it is a five-star hotel.

THE INDEX TOWER
This skyscraper is 328 m high and has 80 floors. The first 25 are dedicated to offices. The remaining ones are destined to residential apartments.

DUBAI MALL
With an area equivalent to 50 football fields, it is the world's largest shopping mall. It has over a thousand stores.

Rapid growth

Satellite photos show the rapid growth of Dubai in the last decade. The artificial islands are a highlight, but questioned for affecting marine life, altering currents and eroding beaches excessively.

2000

2005

2010

The self-sustainable home

Climate change and pollution have become global concerns. Therefore, the challenge now is to build buildings with a minimal impact on the environment through the use of natural resources and energy savings.

The passive house

The so-called "passive house" maintains indoor comfort with natural resources such as sunlight, and with good insulation, thus achieving the minimum need for conventional air conditioning systems. It further contemplates the use of more efficient, recycled materials with low emission of greenhouse gases, among others.

AIR EXCHANGE
The stale air passes through a wheel or a structure with overlapping plates, with gaps in between, without mixing with the fresh air.

Fresh air

Foul air

SOLAR PANEL
Photovoltaic panels convert solar energy in electric energy and they can be complemented with other systems.

RAINWATER
One of the systems to seize rain water is the installation of an underground tank that receives rain from the roof drains and then distributes it throughout the house.

EXCHANGERS
They are panels that use solar energy to heat water.

DRY TOILET
It is a toilet with two compartments, to separate excrement. It saves water, avoids contamination of underground soil layers and allows the creation of manure.

GREENHOUSE AND VEGETABLE GARDEN
There is usually a space for growing food. The vegetable gardens in greenhouses allow a varied production throughout the year.

ENERGY SAVING LAMPS
Compact fluorescent lamps use less energy than incandescent lighting and achieve equal levels of lighting.

RECYCLED FURNITURE
The use of paperboard, recycled paper and other materials in the manufacture of furniture is a clear tendency, like reusing antiques.

GLASS SURFACES
The large windows are oriented towards where the sun shines for most part of the day so as to allow the entry of light and heat. The hermetic glass structure reduces the loss of the heat.

Home automation

In recent decades a new type of construction was born called the smart home or domotic house, which integrates several modern technologies to the house. The operation of the apparatus is controlled by software and can be monitored remotely.

Total automation

From a touch screen, usually located near the access door to the house, all movements inside the house and the land surrounding it are scheduled and monitored. In addition, home-owners can monitor the operation of all equipment and systems remotely from any device with Internet access.

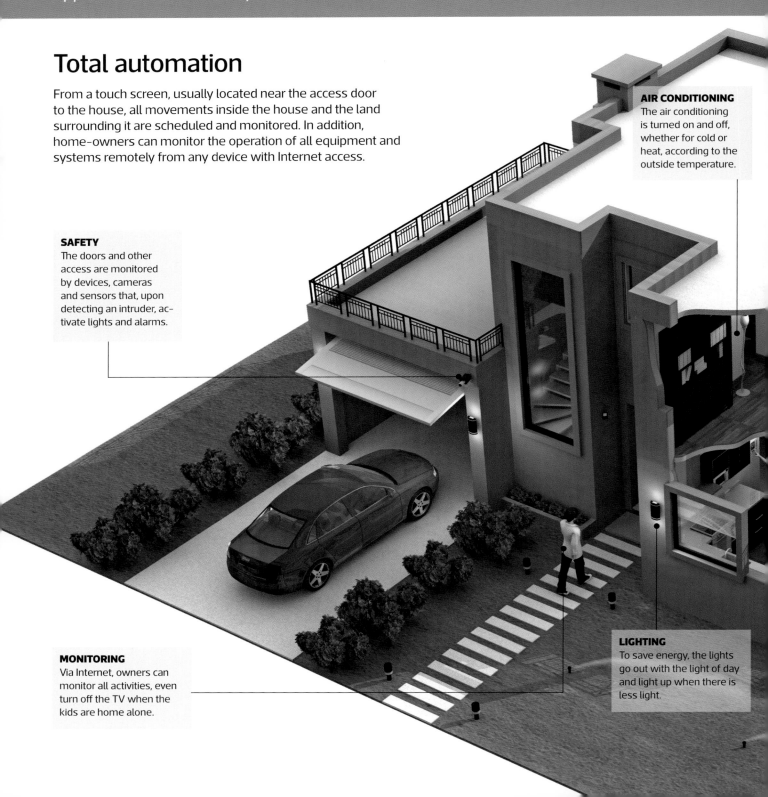

AIR CONDITIONING
The air conditioning is turned on and off, whether for cold or heat, according to the outside temperature.

SAFETY
The doors and other access are monitored by devices, cameras and sensors that, upon detecting an intruder, activate lights and alarms.

MONITORING
Via Internet, owners can monitor all activities, even turn off the TV when the kids are home alone.

LIGHTING
To save energy, the lights go out with the light of day and light up when there is less light.

SCREENS
Daily life and what happens in the rooms appears constantly in the screens located inside the home.

IRRIGATION AND LAWNMOWER
Irrigation is automatically switched depending on weather conditions. The lawnmower runs on a sched- uled basis and charges its battery when it is almost empty.

SWIMMING POOL
Thanks to the drivers installed on it, the water temperature is always ideal. The same applies to the amount of water: it fills and empties automatically.

The domestic robot

These mobile robots are connected to a home automation network. They are mainly used for chores such as vacuuming or cleaning dust, or for security and surveillance.

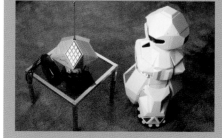

SENSORS
According to the information received by sensors, certain mecha- nisms are activated. For example, in case of rain, the awning is opened or closed depending on whether the presence of a person is detected or not.

SIMULATION
When no one is inside the house, the security system simulates otherwise, for example, it can be programmed to turn the lights on or move the curtains at certain times.

Glossary

ACROPOLIS A fortified part of an ancient Greek city.

AGGLOMERATION A collection of things.

AGRARIAN Relating to the cultivation of land.

ANTECHAMBER A small room leading to a main one.

ANTIQUITY Relating to the ancient past.

BAROQUE Relating to a style of European architecture, music, and art of the 17th and 18th centuries.

BAZAAR A type of Middle Eastern market.

BITUMEN A black substance used for road surfacing and roofing.

BOURGEOIS Relating to middle class materialistic values or conventional attitudes.

CASEMATE A small room in a fortress from which guns or missiles can be fired.

HOMINID A primate of a family (Hominidae) that includes humans and their fossil ancestors.

METROPOLIS The chief city of a country or region.

NEOCLASSICISM The revival of a classical style in art, literature, architecture, or music.

NEOLITHIC Relating to the later part of the Stone Age.

OBSIDIAN A glasslike volcanic rock.

ORTHOGONAL At right angles.

PALAEOLITHIC Relating to the early phase of the Stone Age.

PERISTYLE A row of columns surrounding a space within a building.

POSTERN A back or side entrance.

PROLETARIAT Working-class people.

STRATUM A class to which people are assigned according to their social status, education, or income.

TOPOGRAPHY The natural and artificial physical features of an area.

VESTIBULE A hall or lobby next to the outer door of a building.

ZOOMORPHIC Representing animal forms or gods of animal form.

American Planning Association

205 N. Michigan Avenue, Suite 1200

Chicago, IL 60601-5927

(312) 431-9100

Website: https://www.planning.org

The American Planning Association helps in the development of vital communities by advocating excellence in planning and providing its members with the tools and support necessary to meet the challenges of growth and change.

American Public Works Association

Washington, DC, Office

1401 K Street NW, 11th Floor

Washington, DC 20005

(202) 408-9541

Website: http://www.apwa.net

The American Public Works Association is an international association dedicated to providing high-quality public works goods and services.

Association of Metropolitan Planning Organizations

1730 Rhode Island Avenue NW, Suite 608

Washington, DC 20036

(202) 296-7051

Website: http://www.ampo.org

Established in 1994, AMPO is a nonprofit organization designed to serve the needs and interests of "metropolitan planning organizations (MPOs)" nationwide.

Canadian Institute of Planners

141 Laurier Avenue West, Suite 1112

Ottawa, ON K1P 5J3

(800) 207-2138

Website: http://cip-icu.ca

The Canadian Institute of Planners addresses the use of land, resources, facilities and services in ways that secure the physical, economic and social efficiency, health and well-being of urban and rural communities.

The National League of Cities

1301 Pennsylvania Avenue NW, Suite 550

Washington, DC 20004

(202) 626-3000

Website: http://www.nlc.org

The mission of the National League of Cities is to strengthen and promote cities as centers of opportunity, leadership and governance.

Urban Land Institute

1025 Thomas Jefferson Street NW, Suite 500 West

Washington, DC 20007

(202) 624-7000

Website: http://www.uli.org

Founded in 1936, the Urban Land Institute is a community that fosters the entrepreneurial and collaborative process of real estate development and land use policy-making.

WEBSITES

Because of the changing nature of internet links, Rosen Publishing has developed an online list of websites related to the subject of this book. This site is updated regularly. Please use this link to access the list:

http://www.rosenlinks.com/VHW/cities

Desmond, Matthew. *Evicted: Poverty and Profit in the American City.* New York, NY: Crown Publishers, 2016.

Glaeser, Edward L. *Triumph of the City: How Our Greatest Invention Makes Us Richer, Smarter, Greener, Healthier, and Happier.* New York, NY: Penguin Press, 2011.

Graham, Wade. *Dream Cities: Seven Urban Ideas That Shape the World.* New York, NY: Harper, 2016.

Gravel, Ryan. *Where We Want to Live: Reclaiming Infrastructure for a New Generation of Cities.* New York, NY: St. Martin's Press, 2016.

Jacobs, Jane. *The Death and Life of Great American Cities.* New York, NY: Vintage Books, 1992.

Klein, Gabe. *Start-Up City: Inspiring Private and Public Entrepreneurship, Getting Projects Done, and Having Fun.* Washington, DC: Island Press, 2015.

Koeppel, Gerard T. *City on a Grid: How New York Became New York.* Boston, MA: Da Capo Press, 2015.

Montgomery, Charles. *Happy City: Transforming Our Lives Through Urban Design.* New York, NY: Farrar, Straus and Giroux, 2013.

Schwartz, Samuel I. *Street Smart: the Rise of Cities and the Fall of Cars.* New York, NY: PublicAffairs, 2015.

Townsend, Anthony M. *Smart Cities: Big Data, Civic Hackers, and the Quest for a New Utopia.* New York, NY: W.W. Norton & Company, 2014.

Index